JIHAD:

A Commitment to Universal PEACE

Marcel A. Boisard

American Trust Publications

First published in French under the name
L'Humanisme de L'Islam
by Albin Michel, 1979

This English translation is published by
The American Trust Publications
10900 W. Washington Street
Indianapolis, Indiana 46231

Copyright© American Trust Publications 1988 (1408 H.)

This book is copyright under the Berne Convention
No reproduction without permission
All rights reserved

Library of Congress Cataloguing in Publication Data
87-070337
ISBN 0-89259-073-4
Printed in the United States of America

Table of Contents

The Division of the World. 3

Patience. 11

Effort. 23

Violence. 30

Magnanimity. 40

Eternal Principles. 53

Preface

If Islam is to continue and prevail as the Creator intended—a comprehensive, universal system guiding humanity in all spheres of life, political and economic, moral and ethical, social and esthetic, ritual and spirtual—there must be a renaissance in Muslim thought that articulates and models Islam in its originality, both intellectually and practically. But this flowering will be sterile if it forgets that any literature on Islam requires the medium of a human community to live by and for it in the midst of competing ideologies, sophisticated global circumstances, and the humanistic influences that hold sway in modern times.

Somehow the works of the major contemporary Muslim thinkers in the prevalent languages of the Islamic peoples, though original, did not succeed in inspiring Muslims with the confidence to take Islam and elevate it to the ultimate system of rule in even Muslim societies. Nor have their words convinced those who differ with Islam in thought and creed to accept it or sympathize with its ideals and world view. Indeed, it is questionable whether they made Islam more accessible to the non-Muslim.

As for Western literature on Islam, it differs diametrically in motive and aim from the writings of the Muslim thinkers. Besides being tiny as a corpus, it remains monopolized by orientalists who take Islamic and Arabic studies as a profession, exploiting the hegemony of Western civilization and the prestige of academic institutions whose credentials were established within the realm of the West and in fields other than Islamic studies.

The orientalist positioned himself as the exclusive voice for Western interests, as opposed to the Muslim thinker, and the sole source for interpreting Islam and the aspirations of Muslims, spreading a variety of fictions, biases, and prejudices through primarily unoriginal and non-objective studies.

Recently, however, a few among a new generation of orientalists have had the courage and academic integrity to address Islam as a milestone in the larger edifice of human civilization. Fred Donner of the University of Chicago, for example, in his work *The Early Is-*

lamic Conquests, refuses to adhere to the pat orientalist notion that *jihād* in the formative years of Islam was essentially motivated by desire for worldly gain.

Likewise, in the pages that follow, excerpted from *Humanism in Islam*, Marcel Boisard, approaches *jihād* within the larger context of inter-civilizational relations. Its legitimacy arises in response to the absence of religious freedom and personal security, and the institutionalization of iniquity in society, which Islam views as an inherently less developed—and wholly unacceptable— level of human existence.

There are points where we would disagree with Boisard, for instance, in his assertion that the Qur'ān teaches that Allah in His omnipotence broke the unity of human society for its own good. Allah did not break the unity of society, but instilled it with a natural diversity and variety that facilitates its very organization. the underlying unity of humanity is very much, and quite inherently, intact. Boisard's analysis of a divinely "broken" unity leads him somewhat away from the unicity and elaboration within revelation in general.

Yet *Humanism* in particular, if we are to borrow from Boisard's sincerity, is a sterling example of objectivity, to the degree this is possible, and academic honesty. His rare desire to go beyond occidental apology to the univerality of Islam, the system, revealed to him the complex reality and beauty of Islam, the way of life. He describes with insight the geography of Islamic concetps and their relationship to the world that this religion envisions and seeks to bring about. This is prerequisite for all who aim to understand relations between Muslim and non-Muslim peoples.

In the course of his analysis, Boisard becomes an advocate of genuine Islam's superior ordering of humanity and the activity of life on earth. The book is a milestone in Western literature on Islam and a source of enrichment for the libraries of Muslims and non-Muslims. One who would care to further his or her understanding of international relations in Islam from a purely Muslim intellect would do well to turn to AbdulHamid AbuSulayman's foundational work, *The Islamic Theory of International Relations*, which presents not only a detailed position but prepares an attitude and illustrates a clear methodology.

As Muslims, we are not averse to hearing anyone speak on Islam, so long as a level of intellectual honesty, personal sincerity, and human fairness is maintained. *American Trust Publications* has committed itself to bringing forth works, by Muslims and non-Muslims, that further understanding and deepen awareness about Islam. We would like to be part of Islam's introduction to the English speaking world, believing that it will moderate dialogue between religions, civilizations, and among humanity, and provide the elements of a higher existence so needed by a world in search of meaning.

Ahmad Zaki Hammad, Ph.D
Chairman, Board of Editors
American Trust Publications

Review

"The traditional Western prejudice which portrays Islam as a belligerent religion gave rise to a derogatory and permanent definition of the 'Muslim Holy war.' The term leads us to believe that Muslims are supposedly encouraged to take up arms in order to impose the faith by force, annihilating those who reject it. The generic term jihad means 'effort,' perhaps a violent one, but in no way specifically a military one. Still, in the noninformed public opinion of the West, it seems to have retained only its meaning of war."

In Jihad the Continuing Struggle, Boisard explains, in very precise terms, what Jihad really is. He discusses the fallacies and the falsities that surround the Western understanding and depiction of Jihad. The West continues to refuse to accept that principles based on religion can be brought into the "philosophy of our industrial age." They ignore the fact Islam is not hostility but dynamism, and that 'adl, Ihsan, Musawat – justice, compassion, equality – are the three pillars of healthy human relations for the true believer.

The Qur'ān, at times, sanctions the use of armed conflict as a means to remove oppression, persecution, and injustice. The permission it grants the believers is essentially restricted and limited to the achievement of specific moral objectives. Aggression and initiation of combat without any valid reason is forbidden. In the Qur'ān we find these instructions: "O ye who believe! Stand out firmly for Allah as witnesses to fair dealing, and let not the hatred of others make you swerve to wrong and depart from justice. Be just: that is next to piety: and fear Allah." (5:8)

Again in the Qur'ān we find these instructions: "To those against whom war is made, permission is given to fight (back) because they are wronged." (22:39)

The Qur'ān is also quite explicit on the point that, in fighting, the Muslims must not transgress the bounds of equity and justice. If the enemy is inclined to peace, they must make peace. (Qur'ān 8:61)

Islam stands for all that is good and valuable in life-human dignity, freedom of choice, justice, equality and brotherhood. Whenever these are threatened it becomes a sacred duty of every member of the human race, male or female, to stand up, and if need be fight for that which is, in actuality, a God given right. The Qur'ān explains that oppression is worse than slaughter and we must fight until there is no oppression. (Qur'ān 2:191-193)

The Qur'ān and Islamic doctrine often associate effort and struggle with patience, generosity, and forgiveness. Combative force against those who consciously oppose justice, compassion, and equality is at times neccessary. However, as Boisard points out, "jihad of the sword" cannot be vindictive and, even less, cruel. "Jihad of the heart" tempers the combative force so that the two ways continue to culminate in magnanimity.

The often-quoted instructions of Abu Bakr contain the moral spirit of Islamic law pertaining to "jihad of the sword": "Remember that you are always under the gaze of Allah and at the threshold of your death, and that you will account for your deeds on the Last Day... When you are fighting for the glory of Allah, aquit yourselves as men, without turning your backs; but, let not the blood of women, children, or the aged be a blemish on your victory. Do not destroy palm trees, do not burn houses or wheat fields, never cut down a fruit tree and do not kill cattle unless you are forced to eat them. When you grant a treaty or a capitulation, take care to fulfill their conditions. As you advance, you will come across religious men who live in monasteries and who serve Allah in prayer; leave them in peace, do not kill them and do not destroy their monasteries..."

For those individuals who would like to develop a better understandin of the "Muslim Holy War" or Muslims, this book may offer some new insight. Boisard, inspite of his failure to understand some aspects of Islamic thought, has done an excellent job of explaining jihad. May Allah reward him.

Aminah Janan Assilmi

The Division of the World

As a total divine truth and perfect spiritual ideal, constituting a particular political entity and social organization, Islam is a universal creed based on a profound consciousness of monotheism. While it is the religion of certainty, which directs the conscious energy and will of the believers toward the organization of the earthly world, Islam seems to have revealed the facets of both internationalism and exclusivity. In its turn, the image of the world projected by the religion determines a specific theory of international relations: of either the organization of peace or the state of war. In the final analysis, it also defines rules pertaining to the waging of aggression.

The Qur'ānic revelation and the civilization that it engendered gave rise to a specific view of man and society and contributed in forming a system of rules pertaining to relations between nations. This was done through the new laws it brought and through the transmission of ancient principles which the expanding Muslim world adopted and communicated. These rules and principles have to be put into the specific context of international relations such as Islam conceives them. For the purposes of an essentially theoretical demonstration and as a starting point, we will consider the ideal of a unified, integrated, and uniform Muslim world without taking the historical or contemporary political reality into account.

A question immediately arises: can one abstractly speak of an "international Islamic law"? Islamic law is a rule of action; law is the classification of acts and the evaluation of their consequences. Law is universal since it has in mind all human actions. Thus, one cannot conceive of an "international law" separate from the global Islamic law, founded upon different sources and maintained by particular sanctions. Nonetheless, a specific discipline by the name of *siyar* developed rapidly.[1] Its sources lie primarily in the Qur'ān and traditions. Judicial doctrine did not evolve a general theory of international law as a particular branch of the judicial sciences but rather developed a

---

[1] That is to say "movement" or "behavior." The meaning of the term acquires the restrictive sense of the "conduct" of the Prophet in his wars and, still later, of the conduct of Islamic governments in international affairs. See Muhammad Hamidullah, *Muslim Conduct of State*, 5 rev. ed. (Lahore: Ashraf, 1968), pp. 10-12. After this: Hamidullah, *Muslim Conduct*.

4. . . . . Jihad: A Commitment to Universal Peace

theoretical structure which offered solutions for each analyzed case. In the classical concept, elements of a political or sociological nature were not supposed to play any decisive role. The foundations of the Islamic law of nations are the eternal truth and justice revealed by God. Neither the custom nor the actual practice of political and diplomatic relations constitutes a formal source of the law. This concept is thus quite different from the modern understanding of law in which various international nations establish the future content of the rules, to a large extent determining their meaning.

It is difficult to give a systematic presentation of the Islamic system. This is because, apart from a few exceptions, its sources and documents are to be found scattered in general treatises.[2] Moreover, the distinction between private and public law, as understood by European doctrines, does not exist because of the law's unicity.

In its positive modern conception, international law presupposes the recognition of independent entities with which relations are established on the basis of respect for sovereignty and equality. If the ultimate goal of Islam was to indefinitely extend its geographical boundaries and the application of its judicial rule, then "Islamic international law" would seem eminently temporary. The close ties between the spiritual and the temporal, supported by the claim of universality, would have excluded the coexistence of the Muslim state with other political systems, even though Islam tolerates Christianity and Judaism on a religious level. Similarly, it would seem impossible to accept different Islamic sovereignties as legal entities. The notion of "nationality" would be absent since Islam first of all represents a community of believers rather than an assembly of citizens. Thus, the non-Muslim would turn out to be not so much an enemy as a potential object of submission to the Qur'ānic law. If the non-Muslim notion of state was foreign to Islamic law,[3] then a conclusion could be made that "Muslim international law" does not exist.

The Islamic representation of the universe is simple and strictly logical. The principle of divine unicity and the general conception of universal order both

---

[2]Generally under the chapter of the "holy war" or of "penalties." With the aim of giving an idea of the complexity of the research, we note, for example, that ibn-Taimiyyah, *On Public and Private Law*, pp. 135 f., in explaining the "holy war," successively deals with war, rebellion, prayer, transactions, loyalty to and confidence in God, goodwill toward others, patience, alms, charity and gentleness, pardon, the joy of life, good intentions, and compensation. From there, he proceeds to forbid finding oneself alone with a woman, advises women not to travel alone for a time span of two days or longer, and he prohibits the libertine of having elegant and beardless servants, etc.

[3]Louis Milliot, *Introduction a l'étude du Droit musulman* (Paris: Sirey, 1953), pp. 779 f. After this: Milliot, *Introduction*; and Majid Khadduri, "The Islamic Theory of International Relations and its Contemporary Relevance" J. Harris Proctor, *Islam and International Relations*, ed. (London: Pall Mall, 1965), pp. 24-39. After this: Khadduri, "The Islamic Theory."

The Division of the World. 5

imply the existential unity of the world. The Qur'ān teaches that God in His omnipotence decided that for the good of humanity the unity of society should be broken: "O mankind! We created you from a single (pair) of a male and a female, and made you into nations and tribes, that you may know each other."[4] Thus, the universe constitutes a unique entity, though from the inside it appears pluralistic, as a collection of diverse communities, in submission to varying laws revealed by God through chosen prophets: "Unto each people is given a guide."[5] In spite of many warnings, the nations have not always respected the law which has been prescribed for them. Muhammad, the seal of the prophets, brought the final message in order to correct the errors or malpractices which had appeared in preceding messages and to complete the transmission of the divine law. This conception is important in the context of international relations because of its threefold consequence. Theoretically speaking, pagans or polytheists did not receive any benefit from the rules which determined relations between peoples unless they showed aggression to Islam. The nations who could justify the source of their beliefs as coming from a book of divine origin were accepted. This recognition is moreover all-encompassing since "there exists no community which has not been visited by a messenger (of God)."[6] Finally, the third and most important consequence from the point of view of inter-community relations was that since Islam claimed to bring the definitive laws and restore universal order, it stood as a world ideology.

The Muslim world, ruled by a formal divine law[7] of universal vocation,[8] had to define the kinds of relations which it was able to maintain with neighboring nations. As a highly structured state and the propagating mechanism of a total conception of the world, it was necessarily going to collide head-on with Christianity, which is also a social and political entity having its own universal and imperialistic claims, despite its internal divisions. This phenomenon is the domain of history.

According to classical Muslim doctrine, the earth is divided into two "worlds": the "world of Islam" and the "world of war." There is nothing unusual about this bipolar conception which does not have any particular importance in itself. In fact, the notion of states as sovereign political entities had not been defined at that time. In theory, a non-Muslim society did not claim judicial equality or even the formal recognition of its existence before attaining a certain level of civilization. This meant being won over to the idea

---

[4] al-Hujurat: 13 (Masson).
[5] ar-Ra'd: 7 (Masson).
[6] Fātir: 24 (Masson).
[7] As in Judaism.
[8] As in Christianity.

6. .... Jihad: A Commitment to Universal Peace

of divine unicity and to have ceased representing a potential danger for the Muslim community. This conception is in no way an extravagant one. The principle of excluding from society peoples of such nations who still have to attain an adequate level of development according to the norms of a certain civilization[9] is fully alive in the twentieth century. Whereas the criteria of evaluation were material in the West, in the Muslim perspective they happen to be spiritual. However, the theoretical aspects pertaining to the apparent makeup of the two "worlds," as well as the principles governing their mutual relationships, make it possible to define the foundations of the Islamic concept of international relations.

In opposition to the "house of Islam"[10] stands the "house of war."[11] In their literal meaning, these names could at first sight lead us to believe that the world is [in the Islamic concept] clearly and irrevocably divided into the Muslim community and the mass of non-believers. In addition to this, they also seem to suggest mutual relations necessarily based on violence. This impression is further reinforced by the subsequent definition of a third division, the "house of reconciliation."[12] This latter division is the specific designation for those non-Muslim states which maintain peaceful relations with Islam, or better still, the territories of protected populations and tributaries of Islam. In order to have a clear understanding of these concepts, it is necessary to give a precise definition which would remove the confusion so often caused by the use of terminology.

In the "house of Islam," Muslim laws and traditions are established and respected. The great majority of the community's members have embraced the faith, and all monotheistic minorities, having accepted the capitation tax, enjoy consequent protection. Since the divine law is applied, all individuals in the "house of Islam," both Muslim and *dhimmi*, are guaranteed security. Thus, the "house of Islam" is also the "house of peace"[13] or the "house of justice."[14] This is the realm of law, order, and harmony. The religious connotation obviously arises from the fact that the Qur'ānic revelation simultane-

---

[9]See Ghoneimi, *The Muslim Conception*, pp. 129-130 f. This author states that the classic Islamic theory of demanding the acceptance of monotheism without insisting upon the adoption of Islam shows itself to be more tolerant than the former doctrine of the West, of which the exclusive criterion of recognition was belonging to Christianity.

[10]*Dar al-Islam*. We prefer the phrase "world of Islam" to the generally used phrases of "house," "abode," or "domain of Islam" because they correspond more exactly to the literal translation of *dar* by reproducing less precisely its political meaning.

[11]*Dar al-Harb*

[12]*Dar al-Sulh*.

[13]*Dar as-Salam*.

[14]*Dar al-'Adl*.

The Division of the World..7

ously offers the faith and the law, respect for which necessarily implies peace and justice. This is the world of Islam. Hence, the primary reality upon which the definition is based is not the religion of the population but the existence of specific institutions and the application of particular rules. The definition's corresponding criterion is the security enjoyed by the inhabitants. The house of Islam, as opposed to the house of war, is thus characterized by the laws which the individual applies and the resulting security which he experiences. A country can be called Islamic if, first of all, the laws it applies are Islamic, and if, secondly, the Muslims and protected minorities enjoy security and the liberty to practice their religion, whether individually or collectively.[15] In the opposing case, the country is considered hostile, belonging to the "house of war," even if it claims to be Muslim and regardless of what the religion of its inhabitants may be. This double condition provides an interesting definition since it reveals the underlying concept of war in Islam. Furthermore, it corresponds to the deeper spirit of the religion, even though certain Muslim jurists or certain Western Islamologists have refuted it, and even though it has been belied by historical events.

The concept of the "houses" is essentially theoretical and primarily juridical. The geographical definition of the "realm of Islam" and its internal divisions seems to be of no real importance, all the more so since the law of rights is "personalized" and not territorial in Islam. A concise description will thus suffice. For most Muslim authors, the sanctified territory surrounding Makkah[16] is reserved exclusively for believers; the Hijaz represents a second division into which non-Muslim monotheists are permitted to go without, however, being allowed to live there permanently. The remainder of the "house of Islam," the largest geographical category, is open without restriction to the "People of the Book" who are allowed to live there as protected persons, or to travel there as foreigners in possession of a travel permit. Since they were first and foremost the product of doctrinal elaboration and the result of historical events or of psychological considerations, these mental geographical divisions were in no way detrimental to the definition of the "world of Islam," nor did they influence international relations.

The "world of war" is not supposed to group all non-Muslim states together. Under certain conditions these states may on the contrary by right and in reality enjoy legitimate existence and total independence. The world of war

---

[15]Ghoneimi, *The Muslim Conception*, p. 156; and Majid Khadduri, *The Islamic Law of Nations*, translation of Shaybani's Siyar (Baltimore: Johns Hopkins, 1966), pp. 218-219. After this: Khadduri, *The Islamic Law*, which is the introduction pp. 1-74 and Shaybani's Siyar, for the translation pp. 75-292.
[16]*Haram*.

8. .... Jihad: A Commitment to Universal Peace

is characterized by the absence of institutions whose function it is to establish peace and justice and also by the nonobservance of the Qur'ānic rule and spirit. It is the reign of violence, ignorance, and tyranny, and is thus identified with the "world of injustice."[17] In the generally accepted term, the word "war"[18] itself takes on a specific meaning. It refers to a situation held to be objective, under the elucidation of Islam's religious and juridical canons. Considered from within, it means war in the genre of anarchy, tension, and disharmony. The "world of war" is opposed to the "world of Islam" by its own institutions, but nothing implies *a priori* that the Muslim should necessarily declare war against this world in order to impose Islam. This bipolar division of the world expresses a struggle between two systems which are opposed by nature – a struggle between justice and injustice, good and evil. In the "world of war," the law applied authorizes oppression, violence, tyranny, and religious coercion. It also permits usury, gambling, alcoholic drinks and any other activity considered to be reprehensible by Muslim morality. Such a state is identified with the "world of war" even if its leaders claim to be Muslims.

The quality of the laws governing a society constitutes the first criterion of the definition. The second deals with the safety of the believers. Those territories in which the Muslim cannot outwardly practice his religion belong to the "world of war." In this respect, Islam guarantees the security of the monotheistic minorities under its protection. The formal recognition of Islam, implying the guaranteed freedom of any person to embrace the faith and to observe its ritual obligations, excludes a country from the "world of war," even if the governmental authority is non-Muslim.

The third and final definition touches upon a more concretely definable reality, geographical in essence. In effect, any neighboring and contiguous territories of the "world of Islam" into which entry is forbidden to Muslims and from which military attacks could at any moment be launched[19] are considered to be a part of the "world of war."

At this stage, we should emphasize three important characteristics. On one hand, the definition of the "world of war" is singularly restrictive since the conditions of evaluation and classification are only cumulatively valid. If one of the conditions is absent, the territory under consideration could not be taken to be an enemy. Furthermore, the basic values of appreciation, the quality of the laws applied, and the security of the believer show that the division

---

[17] *Dar al-Zawr.*
[18] *Harb* as opposed to *Jihad.*
[19] Mohammad Abu Zahra, *La Conception de la guerre dans l'Islam* [The concept of war in Islam] (Cairo: Supreme Council of Islamic Affairs, n.d.), pp. 41 f. After this: Abu Zahra, *La Conception.*

The Division of the World..................................9

of the world in the Islamic concept is not geographical, as has often been claimed in the West.[20] It is true that some Muslim political leaders seized the opportunity so as to justify their desire for expansion, thus helping to give credence to this idea. It is still true, though, that the geographical distinctions and juridical definition do not coincide. In effect, "Islam recognizes two large divisions of humanity: the one branch comprises those who are the true servants of God and champions of the truth, while the other includes those who pursue evil and are champions of error. Islam declares itself in a state of war against all those who constitute the latter category."[21] Since the "world of war" is thus considered because of the iniquity of its institutions and because of the persecution of believers, there immediately appear great possibilities of adaptation and harmony. As a last resort, peaceful coexistence is determined by the very evolution of the "world of war." The hostility of the "world of Islam" ceases when injustice and persecution cease. Of course, the superiority of the Qur'ānic law is never questioned any more than Islam's claim to universality has ceased. However, a non-Muslim country which does not threaten the community of believers and which possesses institutions enforcing the respect of justice and guaranteeing freedom of worship, would be considered as not belonging to the "world of war." Consequently, pacific relations based on integrity and mutual recognition should be able to evolve. Interpretation has greatly varied with the course of history, and such variations often happened during fluctuations in the military and political strength of the Muslims. Still, they were always the deeds of men.

From this point of view, it could seem superfluous to mention the third section of the divided world: the "world of reconciliation"[22] or of "alliance."[23] In effect, it seems hard to understand how a third category could be logically fitted into the bipartite division of the universe. Again, the definition of this latter "world" does not appear very clearly.[24] It is, moreover, a later contribution and seems to be the bequest of a single school of law.[25] However, it is of twofold interest to analyze this category since, first, this could give a better understanding of the bipolar Muslim conception of the world and, second because it shows the possibility for Islam to establish relations with non-Muslim states, devoid of subjection and hostility.

---

[20] Lammens, *L'Islam*, pp. 82-83, among others.
[21] Abul Hassan A. Nadawi, *Islam and the World*, translated from the Arabic by M. Asif Kidwai, 2nd ed. (Lahore: Ashraf, 1967), p. 142. After this: Nadawi, *Islam*.
[22] *Dar al-Sulh*.
[23] *Dar al-Ahd*.
[24] Did the "People of the Book" understand that they had signed a pact of allegiance and accepted the capitation tax or is it rather a case in which the territories or states voluntarily maintained peaceful ties with Islam, or does the term cover both instances?
[25] The Shafi'i school.

10. Jihad: A Commitment to Universal Peace

Since it is possible to envisage a "world of neutrality,"[26] it would be of interest within the context of the system as a whole to enumerate its legal foundations and historical causes. Muslim legal theory recognizes three kinds of neutrality which are confirmed in political practice: Ethiopia, Nubia, and Cyprus.[27] The particular status granted these three countries has its origins respectively in the benevolent attitude of the Ethiopian king toward the Prophet Muhammad and his first companions; in military considerations, such as the inaccessibility of Nubia; and in international rivalry in the case of Cyprus. It is thus undeniable that psychological, practical, military, or diplomatic reasons have played their role. Nonetheless, the basic legal principles seem to have been respected.

Ethiopia was saved from Islamic hostility because first of all it opposed the persecution of believers from the very earliest days, offering asylum to the Muslims who had fled Makkah. Second, the Ethiopian king had recognized the legitimacy of the Qur'ānic law and Muhammad's prophethood. The treaty between Nubia and the Muslim state primarily aimed at putting an end to constant mutual hostility. It appears as a document concluded between two states which reciprocally recognized each other's neutrality, and whose clauses took on an essentially commercial form. However, one of the main clauses deserves special mention since it concerned freedom of conscience and religion.[28] As for Cyprus, it was never a part of either of the "worlds," but was simultaneously subjected to a double allegiance to both Byzantium and Islam. The Cypriots recognized the legitimacy of Muslim law and for a time paid a tax to the Umayyads.

These three examples illustrate and strengthen the theory which claims that the bipartite division of the world and the virtual hostility which it seems to imply are not based on geographical criteria but are determined by the conditions mentioned above: justice, security, and freedom of conscience for the Muslims. There is a certain kind of specialized literature[29] which tries to give credit to the idea that neutrality is a concept foreign to Islam. This assertion represents the conclusion of an analysis which is primarily based on the idea of unyielding antagonism between the Muslim community and the rest of the world. However, neutrality ought to be the normal state of relations if one keeps to the classical definitions of the "worlds" of Islam and of war.

---

[26]*Dar al-Hiyad.*
[27]Khadduri, *War*, pp. 252-267. Again, was it that the countries which enjoyed the status of neutrality directed no aggression against Islam? This seems, unfortunately, no longer to be the case with Ethiopia.
[28]It stipulates, besides, that the Nubians were authorized to build a mosque in their capital.
[29]See, above all, Khadduri, *War.*

Patience.. 11

Moreover, the Qur'ān considers this case.[30] It is true that the traditional doctrine offers little information and does not give a systematic description of the rights and duties emanating from the status of neutrality whose legal conception, in any event, appeared only recently. A specifically Islamic theory has yet to be codified, based upon scanty doctrinal references and pertaining especially to practice.[31]

The matter of relations between Islam and non-Muslim peoples has been the object of numerous contradictory discussions which have more than mere theoretical value since they determine the possible legitimacy of armed conflict and thus, indirectly, the rules pertaining to the conduct of aggression. The division of the world is an incontestably yet not exclusively Islamic concept. More recently, it has been claimed[32] that it was the product of reflections of certain jurists who based their arguments on Muhammad's order to the first believers to leave Makkah, the "land of war," in order to make for Medinah, the "land of Islam." The division of the world, according to them, is not advocated either by the Qur'ān or the traditions, and the emigration of the first believers nullifies distinctions and dissipates all contempt.

Such a point of view of course does not correlate with the true spirit of Islam and disregards the near absoluteness of Muslim doctrine on this matter. The question presents itself in a different perspective, which is in fact practical and ultimately more interesting. Do relations between the "world of Islam" and the "world of war" necessarily have to be governed by permanent hostility, marked by armed conflicts interspersed with temporary truces,[33] or can they, on the contrary, remain pacific, thanks to the concept of the existential unity and order of the world as well as to the recognition and respect of the revelations preceding Islam? This question will be the object of discussion of the following section.

Patience

The revelation creates for the believers a spiritual, psychological, and legal bond of a religious nature. According to the jurists of classical Islam, it

---

[30] Particularly an-Nisa': 90: "Except for this law those who would have sought refuge with your allies and those who march against you, sad at heart of having to fight against you or against their own people. If God had wanted, had it pleased Him, He could have given them power over you, and they would have fought you. If these people withdraw from you, if they do not fight against you, if they offer you peace, God does not allow any act of hostility against them," (Reda).
[31] Hamidullah, *Muslim Conduct*, on pp. 283 f. blazes some interesting trails in this direction.
[32] Bêchebichy, *Les relations*, p. 20.
[33] Lammens, *l'Islam*, pp. 82-83 and Khadduri, *War*, whose idea is the very thesis of the book.

moreover implies the necessity of establishing a solid and autonomous Muslim state as a body which applies the divine laws, subjecting both society as a whole and the individual: believers or protected "People of the Book." The imperative existence of a state, based on a faith both universalist and proselitic, engendered a certain philosophy of relations with the outside world which was theoretically maintained until the abolition of the caliphate in 1924.

For Islam as for any other state or system, the organization and quality of relations with neighboring peoples were largely conditioned in practice by its geographical position and its military power which evolved with the course of history. The foundations of "foreign policy" could be found in the Qur'ānic revelation itself. As an "intermediate nation"[34] on the geographical and cultural levels, the Islamic community was obliged to maintain the most cordial relations possible with contiguous states. The idea of "intermediate" goes beyond the strictly geographical notion, assuming a moral, individual, and collective meaning – that is, connotations of prudence, equilibrium, and moderation.[35] Nonetheless, the question arises as to whether the universal calling of Islam, implemented by a state symbolizing a tool for spreading the faith, allows for coexistence with neighboring nations, and especially with those systems which also have claims to internationalism. On a religious level, it was by accepting the preceding divine revelations that Islam appeared to acknowledge the legitimate existence of foreign states on a political level and in accordance with the community concept of that period. The Qur'ān, in essence, cast the foundations of a pacific system of relations on an almost planetary scale when it asserted that each nation had received its own divine "warning."[36]

Even though the Qur'ān at times violently attacks the Jews and, to a lesser degree, the Christians, accusing them of falsifying the scriptures, it does not in any way pronounce a judgment of exclusion upon them. On the contrary, it seems to explicitly guarantee the legitimacy and rights of various societies to exist.[37] Thus, the principles governing international relations must have been immediately very liberal since they admitted the existence of "foreign entities" in a large universal community of nations. The prophetic traditions report many examples confirming Qur'ānic instructions. For example, when

---

[34]al-Baqarah: 143.
[35]Nation "stretched to the extremes" according to the translation of Blachère.
[36]Muhammad Ali, *The Prophet of Arabia* (Beirut: Khayats, n.d.), see the last page.
[37]"Among His signs are the creation of the heavens and the earth, and the variations in your languages and your colors. Verily, there are signs here for those who know," ar-Rum: 22 (Masson). The term "sign" is here understood in the sense of "proof."

Patience..13

he received the representatives of the Christian community of Najran, Muhammad reproached them for claiming that Christ was divine and invited them to become Muslims. However, he did not exert any pressures on them whatsoever but, on the contrary, placed his mosque in Medinah at their disposal so that they could pray there according to their faith. He concluded a treaty with them, three points of which deserve mention. First, the agreement had no time limit. Second, the allowances offered and requested by the young Muslim state seemed equitable: that the Najranites furnish clothing, arms, and mounting horses in the event of a foray into the Yemen, and that they receive and put up any Muslim emissary for the period of one month. In return, Muhammad guaranteed the protection – at no expense of military service or tithe – of the state, the persons, possessions, and religion of the Najranites. Finally, the negotiations had taken place between two powers which mutually considered each other as equals: one, Najran, artisans; the other, Medinah, military.[38]

On the legal level, there are numerous and oftentimes violent debates as to the possibility of formal recognition of foreign states by Islam. Some non-Muslim writers claim that the countries constituting the "world of war" lack the legal means of truly being subjects of Muslim international law; they could only be the objects thereof, owing to certain humanitarian attitudes. On the contrary, modern Muslim authors believe that Islam – which most definitely did not invent anything new in the realm of international relations – was nevertheless the first coherent legal system to assert the notion of a total acknowledgment of exterior political entities[39] and which, on the basis of a sacred duty, guaranteed rights to foreign peoples in times of war as in times of peace.

Modern terminology is not compatible with the terms of the divine revelation and thus renders any comparative analysis difficult. Since the contemporary international system is founded upon the theoretical concepts of equality and reciprocity, the question arises as to whether these conditions can be fulfilled by traditional Islamic legislation which aims at universality. Muslims reply in the affirmative, arguing that the rule of divine law should most certainly be established throughout the entire world and by any means, especially by peaceful methods[40] since the religion could not be imposed by force.[41] In

---

[38] Massignon, *Parole donnée*, p. 159 which is cited besides in this regard an author less favorable to Islam than Lammens.
[39] Hamidullah, *Muslim Conduct*, p. 68. The problem of establishing diplomatic relations is different, as, for example, the position of Saudi Arabia vis-à-vis the Soviet Union.
[40] al-'Ankabut: 46.
[41] al-Baqarah: 256.

14. .... Jihad: A Commitment to Universal Peace

their opinion, the Qur'ānic revelation confirms the principle of nationalities,[42] preaches peace, and demands scrupulous respect of treaties. On the level of doctrine, international law was established so as to define the rights and duties of foreign states since the founders of the system considered the Muslim community as a unique whole.[43] Different forms of mediation, arbitration, and negotiation were recognized and practices systematized.

The manner in which the Prophet and his successors addressed the kings and leaders of non-Muslim peoples shows that they treated them as equals. The minutely elaborate procedure regulating the status of ambassadors and envoys is another expression of this behavior, over and above the immunities and tax exemptions, on the condition that there be reciprocity. It was on an identical basis of reciprocity that an Islamic commercial international law was founded. These premises, selected from among others, constitute convincing arguments, especially if one emphasizes the fact that the myth of the legal equality of states is a recent concept which had not been defined by any of the ancient systems of law. History shows that the Muslim authorities, without renouncing the universality of Islam, were bound by a certain number of specific legal obligations in their dealings with foreign nations. By contrast, it was not until the middle of the nineteenth century that the Ottoman Empire was acknowledged by the West, out of respect for the law of nations, and with several reservations due to the "barbaric humanity" of this empire!

Embassies were already established in the time of the Prophet immediately after the creation of the Islamic community at Medinah. Sometimes their specific aims were to conclude an armistice, peace, or negotiations for the exchange of prisoners. Many of these missions also aimed at inviting the outside world to embrace Islam and could thus have assumed the character of a notification of aggression[44] leading either to an armed conflict or to the signing of a treaty of capitulation. The time span of history, ignorance of the true facts, and the evolution of the minds of men should nevertheless not lead to erroneous conclusions. The enthusiastic energy of the first Muslims and the consequent hostility of the tribes of the Arabian peninsula produced conflicts which could be considered as attempts at "discussion" or as legitimate defense. Of course, one particular Muslim faction, the Kharijites, claimed that force rather than persuasive discussion should be used in order to impose upon nonbelievers the true faith and law capable of routing evil and estab-

---

[42] al-Baqarah: 62 and al-Hujurat: 13.
[43] Hamidullah, *Muslim Conduct*, pp. 72-73.
[44] Khadduri, *War*, p. 245. We specify that the call became a notification of hostilities if the foreigner showed himself hostile to Islam since there is "no compulsion in religion," al-Baqarah: 256.

Patience..15

lishing justice. In this respect, it was not difficult for them to quote Qur'ānic verses taken out of context. The disappearance of this party as a political force and the extinction of the ideas it propagated, at a time when the Muslim state was rapidly expanding and becoming a great military force, prove that Islam opposed fanaticism in its own cradle. At the present time, numerous Muslim authors[45] explain that, in the true spirit of Islam, the basis of relations between Muslims and other peoples is peace. Qur'ānic quotations,[46] legal interpretations, and historical illustrations abound in their writing.

Two examples – one individual, the other collective – may serve to illustrate Islam's "recognition" of foreign political entities: the safeguard guaranteed all foreigners and the procedure regulating the conclusion of treaties.

The original system of protection granted to non-Muslims traveling in Islamic territory openly proves that Islamic doctrine never preached the extermination of nonbelievers. This principle was legally formulated from the time of the revelation itself; its spirit has remained in Islamic political morals. European travelers were highly impressed by this, as is indicated in their reports, particularly in the eighteenth century. The "foreigner" is the nonbeliever. Since he is a member of a country not ruled by Islamic law, and hence of the "world of war," he has a special status. He is not considered as an enemy since, according to the Muslim notion, war is against governments and not against peoples. Even in a period of hostilities between Islam and the territory from which he comes, it is always possible for him and his family to enter, travel, and temporarily reside in the Muslim world without danger or any harrassment. The safeguard granted to him makes him the beneficiary[47] of a recognition of his personality and guarantees the security of his person and property. His treatment is regulated in strict accordance with the Qur'ānic faith or else, should such a case be necessary, according to the clauses of a possible treaty uniting Islam and the individual's country of origin. The judicial basis of this institution is not without a prosyletic spirit: "If one among the pagans ask you for asylum, grant it to him, so that he may hear the word of God; and then escort him to where he can be secure. That

---

[45] Abu Zahra, *La Conception*; Bêchebichy, *Les relations*; Amir Ali, *The Spirit*; Katirjoglou, *La Sagesse*, for only a limited number of citations.
[46] "If they [the non-Muslim] incline toward peace, incline toward them ..." al-Anfal: 61 (Blachère). Or again: "O you who believe! When you engage yourselves in the cause of God, investigate carefully, and do not say to anyone who offers you a salutation: (you are not a believer!) coveting the goods of the life of this world. The spoils are abundant with God! Not long ago you also were in the same situation, but God conferred on you His favor. Therefore, carefully investigate before you condemn. God is well aware of all that you do," an-Nisa': 94 (Reda).
[47] *Mustamin*.

16. . . . . Jihad: A Commitment to Universal Peace

is because they are men without knowledge."[48] On the level of practice, the rights granted to a foreigner who enjoys the privilege of security depend on the kind of relationship which he has established with the Muslim world – that is, temporary and occasional. Other than the protection of his person and property, he enjoys the right to practice his religion, to remain subordinate to his own national legislation, and to indulge in trade within the confines of the law. He conversely has the duty of respecting the Islamic religion and the person of its Prophet, of not causing public disturbance, and to leave the territory upon the expiration of his permit. Should he violate any laws of conduct – that is, if he commits a penal error, the protection remains valid but does not acquit him of whatever punishment the law has provided. Reciprocally, if he were to be the victim of a Muslim, the latter would be punished by the leader of the community or his representative since the safeguard engages the responsibility of both the community and of all the believers individually.

The formalities according to which the permit is granted are reduced to their simplest expression. If the intention of the nonbeliever is clear, a greeting or even a simple gesture are sufficient. The safety of the foreigner who thus enters into Islamic territory is absolutely guaranteed since the institution draws its force from the divine law. It could not be subject to the ever possible fluctuations in the legislation of man. The foreigner becomes a sanctified guest. If for some imperative reason the safeguard were to be broken, the beneficiary enjoys the absolute right of being re-escorted without violence to the boundaries of the state from which he comes. This institution, considered to be the living expression of Islamic tolerance and sanctified hospitality, is in fact much more. In a certain sense, the right of anybody to offer asylum on behalf of the society as a whole is a sort of individual manifestation against the authority of the leader and against the mystical community bond.[49] It thus illustrates above all else the intrinsic respect which Islam shows for the individual.

Upon expiration of the permit, which cannot exceed a year, the foreigner returns home or else remains in Muslim territories. In such a case, he is permitted to live indefinitely in the "world of Islam," thus becoming a "protected person,"[50] subject to tax, integrated into the community of those whose faith he shares and subordinate to its social laws. By virtue of these terms which

---

[48]at-Taubah: 6 (Abbasi).
[49]One could equally make the opposite deduction, namely that it is a case of an individual manifestation of the collective responsibility, by which the leader himself is obligated to and reinforces the communal mystic tie.
[50]*Dhimmi*.

facilitate the permanent settling of foreigners wishing to leave their country for one reason or another, the Muslim community soon appeared as a virtual place of asylum and refuge. From this point of view, it seems obvious first of all that Islam "grants" rights to individuals coming from foreign countries and, second, that the prohibition for Muslims to form friendships with Jews and Christians[51] can be understood only insofar as such a relationship could threaten the faith of the believer or bring harm to the community. The Qur'ān in any case clearly indicates this: "O you who believe! Take not for friends and protectors those who take your religion for a mockery or sport, whether among those who received the Scripture before you, or among those who reject faith..."[52] Not only do the prophetic traditions show this while history proves it, but the Qur'ān orders it. The Muslim must in fact be generous toward a foreigner who is not hostile toward him. Thus, fruitful and permanent ties were established on the levels of both commercial relations and cultural exchange. Whatever the international situation may have been, the doors of the Islamic world remained wide open to non-Muslim travelers, refugees, and merchants.

However, this institution did not only have proselytizing aims. Wishing to escape isolation and ignorance, the believers drew from the most diverse sources of knowledge. By soliciting amicable relationships, the Muslims contributed to the development of their community and at the same time brought about an immense stirring of peoples and ideas. Thus, they contributed to the rise of a brilliant civilization which developed in subsequent centuries, spreading into three continents. In this context, numerous were those who, right from the beginnings of Islam, traveled to foreign countries: merchants for business, scholars seeking documents to translate, travelers in pursuit of their own pleasure, missionaries to convey the Qur'ānic message, and so on. The laws to which they still submitted showed that Islam recognizes the validity of foreign legislatures. Having left the "realm of Islam," Muslims were obliged both by legal doctrine and by their religious ethics to abide by the laws of the country where they were stationed and to fully observe the conditions of the permit which they had been granted. Of course, this was the case inasmuch as they would not have to violate the principles of their faith in order to do so. Moreover, they remained bound by the contracts they had concluded with the foreigners before leaving Muslim territory.

---

[51]"O you who believe, do not make ties of friendship with the Jews and the Christians. They are friends, protectors of each other (against you) ..." al-Ma'idah: 51 (Abbasi). The translator states that this verse was revealed after the year 5 A.H., after the Jews and the Christians had together shown themselves hostile to Islam.
[52]al-Ma'idah: 57 (Masson).

18. Jihad: A Commitment to Universal Peace

Of course, the institution of safeguard existed before Islam. At all times, nations have felt the need to maintain nonbelligerent relations with their neighbors. The Muslims, however, were to make this a principle which would be enforced throughout the state, giving it a sacred value, facilitating and extending the field of its application. This development attained such a point that the safeguard is sometimes considered to be an original Islamic institution. Historically, it has played an important role by making temporary though frequent individual contacts between the world of Islam and the outside world. It also allowed for an extensive pacific exchange of people and ideas, techniques and products. Finally, by providing security to foreign envoys on assignment (in the world of Islam), it laid the foundations of diplomatic activities which soon became established between the Islamic state and its neighboring countries.

The treaties provide the second concrete example which illustrates the Islamic practice of international relations. The treaty of Hudaibiyah was the first "interstate" pact which the Muslims concluded with the Makkan aristocracy. It consecrated the birth of the Islamic state under the direction of Muhammad, simultaneously recognizing Islam as the official religion professed by this authority. Henceforth, the community of believers was going to have to define the policy of its relations with the outside world.

The process was identical to that which, at all times and in different parts of the world, brought about the beginnings of international communities. The proximity of different institutions, as well as the necessity of the coexistence of oftentimes hostile societies, create obligations which over time crystallized into legal norms. The motivations behind such a situation may be material interest, ethical considerations, or the fear of retaliation. The principles behind the application of the rules may vary according to political or social evolution, both in the country under consideration and in the neighboring entities, or these principles may vary in accordance with the equality or disparity in military forces and with the evolution of public and private consciousness. It is therefore extremely hazardous to venture historical parallels since comparisons become meaningless when too great a time span separates the facts under consideration. On the other hand, the basic norms which hold the system together are bound to remain, and it is from this point of view that the Muslim political philosophy concerning treaties and conventions should be analyzed.

The quality of a treaty depends on the theoretical concept of international relations, and on the consideration given to the negotiating party, and to the legal terms enforcing respect for these clauses. Islamic legislation distinguishes three types of treaties according to their aim: the peace treaty, the treaty of protection, and the treaty of ransom. The conventions of peace and

Patience...19

armistice derive their legality from Qur'ānic terms and attitudes as well as from the prophetic traditions.

There are three conditions of validity binding on the treaties. First of all, the clauses may not violate the precepts of Islam nor may they harm the Muslim community. Second, the terms of the agreement must be formulated concisely and with care and must formally define the rights and duties of the contracting parties.[53] The treaties concluded by the Prophet constituted a kind of example or archetype. Even though their content changed over the course of Muslim history,[54] their form remained perceptibly similar. Finally, the third condition of validity is that the treaty express the perfect accord of the signing parties. Here we have an essential order which proves that the contractual spirit of Islam in no way means the unilateral imposition of Muslim claims over an opposing party. The Qur'ān moreover explicitly accords the "immunity of Allah and His Apostle" to non-Muslims with whom the believers have concluded a treaty. It requires that the Muslims be just toward their partners as long as the latter remain just toward the Muslims.[55]

It is not without value in this context to quote several verses of a single *surah* to show the extent to which the respect of the promise and of signed treaties are sacred in the Qur'ānic teachings:

> Fulfill the covenant of God when you have entered into it, and break not your oaths after you have confirmed them; indeed, you have made God your surety for God knows all that you do.
>
> And be not like a woman who breaks into untwisted strands the yarn which she has spun, after it has become strong. Nor take your oaths to practise deception between yourselves, lest one party should be more numerous than another: for God will test you by this; and on the Day of Judgment, He will certainly make clear to you (the truth of) that wherein you disagree.
>
> And take not your oaths to practise deception between yourselves, with the result that someone's foot may slip after it was firmly planted, and you may have to taste the evil (conse-

---

[53] "And take not your oaths to practice deception between yourselves," an-Nahl: 94 (Blachère). See also al-Ahzab: 70.
[54] There is an evolution of the initially essentially religious aspect to the more political considerations after the establishment of the Islamic empire.
[55] at-Taubah: 1, 4, and 7; see also, for example, al-Anfal: 58, or al-Mumtahanah: 8-9.

20. . . . . Jihad: A Commitment to Universal Peace

quences) of having hindered (men) from the path of God, and a mighty wrath descend on you.

Nor sell the covenant of God for a miserable price: for with God is (a prize) far better for you, if you only knew."[56]

The opinions of Muslim authors differ over the duration of these treaties' validity. All of them, according to the jurists, seem to claim that peace should necessarily assume a temporary nature ranging from two to ten years. This time limit[57] helped to give credit to the idea that Islam could only view its relations with the outside world in terms of permanent hostility. One should, however, take into consideration the fact that first of all, the contracts were indefinitely renewable and that, second, ten years represented a reasonable time period at an era of profound change in the Arab world which led to the formation of new political entities. There is no doubt that Muslim jurists saw in this limitation an opportunity of extending the domination of Islam; a means which the political leaders could have exploited if the need arose. However, even if classical legal doctrine seems to be unanimous on the limitation of the treaties' validity, the Qur'ānic revelation makes no mention of it, nor the traditions of the Prophet indicate any limitation.[58] It is thus in all likelihood a question of primarily academic value which has ceased to matter in the practice of states in our day and age.

On the level of conventional practice, those agreements formally limited in duration[59] seem less numerous and less important than those of unlimited duration. The second international pact concluded by the Islamic community[60] was in no way limited, nor were any of the many treaties signed in the course of history until the official end of the caliphate.[61] Naturally, diplomatic relations gradually developed and concurrently the number of treaties increased. The two main reasons for this most likely lay in the increasing contacts with the Christian West and the fragmentation of the Islamic state, which brought about agreements and alliances determined by political expedience. Such ag-

---

[56] an-Nahl: 91-92, 94-95 (Masson).
[57] This is based on the precedent of Hudaibiyyah.
[58] It should say: "The Byzantines have a sure peace with you, Muslims."
[59] Truce for ten years and ten months accorded by the Mameluke Sultan Baibars, in April 1272, with the Franks and the crusade detachments of England, besieging Saint-Jean d'Acre for example. See René Brousset, *L'épopée des croisades* (Paris: n.p., 1957), pp. 428-429.
[60] Treaty of Najran.
[61] By way of examples: the Peace of 1180 between Saladin and the leper king of Jerusalem Baudouin IV, the Treaty of Commerce of 1535 between the Sublime Porte and the king of France, the Treaty of Paris between the Ottoman Empire and the European powers, the adhesion of the Ottoman Turks to the Conventions of Geneva, and so on.

Patience... 21

reements could, however, not have been concluded without time limits if it had been a matter of some formal and basic condition of Qur'ānic law: the validity of a treaty in time has no influence whatsoever on its value.

Over and above the treaties of capitation with the monotheistic peoples contained within the Islamic state, treaties which oblige the Muslim community as a whole but which engage the responsibility of the individual for protected persons, thereby assuming the character of constitutional guarantees, there is yet a third category of agreements which had in mind more specific objectives such as the ransom of prisoners,[62] the establishment of a temporary truce, and the capitulation and evacuation of strongholds. Others aimed at humanitarian objectives such as the evacuation of the wounded and the guarantee of free passage for religious pilgrimage. This type of treaty naturally was of a temporary nature.

The authority to conclude treaties of international status belonged to the Prophet and then to his successors, the caliphs; with regard to treaties of capitation, such contractual authority was given to the imams since these required a profound knowledge of the precepts of the faith.[63] Nevertheless, executive power was often delegated to military commanders in the field or to the imam's representatives. It was only after ratification, however, that they engaged the responsibility of the Muslim community. An agreement which did not correspond to the basic precepts of the religion could be annulled, on the formal condition that the opposing party was notified and that there be a reasonable period of time before the contract finally ceased to be valid.

The obligating power of the treaties is founded upon a religious constraint which guarantees strict observance of the treaty. Any violation would cause a sanction all the more severe since the duty is sacred, deriving from the Muslim conception of the divine message. The foundation of all moral values lies in fact in God's "covenant" with man: the successive revelations and the Qur'ān, descended through Muhammad. Thus, the first virtue of the believer and the community should be to one's promise. The firm intention to fulfil any obligations made, loyalty, and good faith represent the principles underlying Muslim conduct as well as the basis of the state's political philosophy. According to the Qur'ān, God Himself is "faithful to His promises."

Depending on their aims, the treaties could be either permanent with defeated and subjugated peoples, or else temporary military truces, or specific agreements. Their supposedly temporary character seems to be a conclusion

---

[62]The systematization and the development of which were to have important consequences on the formation of the law of modern war.
[63]Bêchebichy, *Les relations*, pp. 39 f.

22. . . . . Jihad: A Commitment to Universal Peace

of classical juridical speculation for there is nothing which formally stipulates it in the Qur'ān. On the contrary, the example of the Prophet shows that the Pact of Medinah, the first international pact of collective security and the first assertion of the principle of religious freedom, had no time limit. Whatever the case may be, the restrictions in doctrine seem to be the result of a twofold consideration. On the one hand, Islam recommends that treaties be concluded with great caution, proportional to the magnitude of the agreement.[64] On the other hand, the reservation is due to the very idea which Islam held of the outside world, as being potentially dangerous and aggressive in essence. According to classical doctrine, to attribute a permanent value to the treaties would be to contradict the basic principle of the opposition between Islam and the "world of war." In fact, the duration of a treaty of undefined duration depends on how loyal the Muslims are to the conditions of the agreement since the believers are required by their religion to adhere scrupulously to the agreement for as long as their contractual partner does the same. However, if one admits that neither the bipolar division of the world nor the constant hostility between ideological systems is more than a historical or factual statement and in no way a legal justification, then the notion of the precarious nature of treaties collapses because of its lack of notion support. We should finally point out that Islam most probably gave a new dimension to the concept of compulsory respect for treaties by making the terms of such treaties legally binding on a truly religious basis. Since God is in effect considered as a third party in the agreement,[65] any violation, whether individual or collective, implies the distortion of an obligation contracted toward Him.

Islam, hardly less than any other religion or ideological system, has naturally known violence and war. Its political expansion was also to a certain extent achieved by the sword. Man – and not the faith – was the main culprit. Islam should be the religion of justice and compassion.[66] However, this compassion is of a particular nature and is distinct from the principles of Western ethics impregnated by Christianity. Muslim compassion is as much individual as it is collective: it is active rather than passive. It is a communal thing since it not only appears as mercy or charity toward one single individual but is equally expressed in favor of society and particularly toward those who are just. It is active because it allows the use of force to establish fraternity and

---

[64] One could, moreover, make a case here of the fact that modern international law also advances restrictions, through the clause "rebus sic stantibus." Besides, it would be easy to speak ironically on the sort of "perpetual" treaties or alliances which recent history has known.

[65] "Remain loyal to the covenant of God when you have entered into it! Do not violate the oaths after you have solemnly confirmed them and have taken Allah as a guarantor against you!" an-Nahl: 91 (Blachère).

[66] "We sent you [Prophet] only as a [sign of] mercy for the world," al-Anbiyyā': 107 (Blachère).

Effort 23

mutual concord, to do away with evil and to curb injustice. Under its Muslim meaning, virtue is above all engaged and dynamic, having both direction and compulsion.

Effort

The traditional Western prejudice which portrays Islam as a belligerent religion gave rise to a derogatory and permanent definition of the Muslim "holy war." The term leads us to believe that Muslims are supposedly encouraged to take up arms in order to impose the faith by force, annihilating those who reject it.[67] The generic term of *jihad* means "effort," perhaps a violent one, but in no way specifically a military one. Still, in the noninformed public opinion in the West, it seems to have retained only its meaning of war. It is true that this can be explained by psychological and historical reasons. Furthermore, a certain tendency toward demagogy has incited certain contemporary Muslim political leaders to make reference to the "holy war" in its exclusively military meaning, precisely in order to hide their intellectual and administrative bankruptcy.

The exact meaning of *jihad* cannot be explained unless it is put back into the context of Islam as well as into the Islamic philosophy of international relations. The "holy war" is in effect that instrument which, if needs be, must impose the reign of Islam – in other words, peace and justice under the protection of the revealed law – upon a recalcitrant and aggressive "world of war." The Muslim community, in submission to the revealed divine law, is necessarily hostile toward error and injustice. This firm opposition must be concretely manifested in terms of varying efforts, determined and conditioned by the nature of the unbalance to be corrected: personal struggle against one's inner erroneous tendencies; moral combat for the respect of Qur'ānic orders; effort made to spread the religion through a pacific missionary calling[68]; armed aggression in a just war, in the "path of Allah"[69] so as to protect the community and to free isolated believers from persecution. Under such conditions, the "holy war" is in reality an instrument used to impose the "world of Islam," understood as harmony, order and peace, which are both spiritual and material, individual and collective. Yet, this "war" does not have the aim of imposing the religion by force. On the contrary, it demands of the believers that they overcome their inner passions. The "passionate ardor for the

---

[67]See, in particular, Lammens, *L'Islam*, pp. 82 f., as well as Khadduri, *War*, where the idea is even more nuanced.
[68]"... but strive against them [the unbelievers] with the utmost strenuousness, with the Qur'ān," al-Furqān: 52 (Blachère).
[69]al-Baqarah: 190.

24..................Jihad: A Commitment to Universal Peace

cause of Allah"[70] should be no more than the effort to live according to His law and the struggle to have His justice reign.

The effort – a violent one if needs be – to impose order and equity[71] is considered by Islamic legislation to be a fundamental duty. As an obligation of solidarity, as opposed to the "Five Pillars of the Faith" considered to be personal duties, it is seen as one of the principal duties of the community's leader. This collective character corresponds to the religious definition of the Muslim community which "orders good and forbids evil," as well as to its political conception of international relations. On the individual level, the believer is engaged in a permanent "holy war," attempting to check his self-centeredness and follow the prescriptions of the divine revelation. This is a spiritual obligation between him and God. The duty of holy war becomes personal, crystalized on a physical and material plain, when the imam calls upon the believers for the defense of Islam. Only in this perspective does the specifically military aspect of *jihad* appear.

Muslim jurists distinguish four types of "holy war": the war waged by the heart, the tongue, the hand, and the sword.[72] The first of these, the "war of the heart," is the internal spiritual and moral struggle which should lead to man's victory over his ego. This is the most important, the most necessary, and the most meritorious. The "war of the tongue" or of gesture is the effort of calm preaching and of setting edifying moral examples for non-Muslims. Within the society it commits the believer to intervene and struggle in an effort to correct error and enforce good conduct. It contributes to collective stability and moral solidarity. Finally, the "*jihad* of the sword" corresponds exactly to armed conflict with the enemies of the Islamic community and foreign leaders who either persecute the believers or restrict the freedom of conscience of their subjects. It results from the rejection of oppression and from the dynamic conception of justice and mercy.

Muslim doctrine established a hierarchic ordering of values. In effect, the most meritorious *jihad* is the one which we "wage against ourselves," according to the prophetic traditions.[73] This personal effort made to overcome the

---

[70]For the use of the formulation, see ibn-Khaldoun, *Les textes sociologiques et économiques de la Mouqaddima*, translated and annotated by Georges H. Bousquet (Paris: Rivière, 1965), pp. 69 f. After this: ibn-Khaldoun, *Mouqaddima*.
[71]This is the essential theme of the sura entitled *at-Taubah*.
[72]Khadduri, *War*, pp. 56-57.
[73]The Prophet, returning from a military expedition against some neighboring enemies, moreover declared: "We are returning from the small holy war to the grand holy war."

Effort... 25

self is considered to be "the greatest holy war."[74] Thus, an armed holy war is relatively secondary, representing no more than the most concrete manifestation of effort. Yet, it is only this expression of the *jihad* which has ever stuck the Western mind. It is also the only form which discretely enters into the context of the present discussion.

In the limited area of the armed holy war, Muslims not only have the right but the duty to engage defensively in hostilities of six different types: against the enemies of God, for the defense of frontiers,[75] against apostates, and against secessionists,[76] against groups who disturb public security, and against monotheists who refuse to pay the capitation tax. We shall briefly discuss each category.[77]

The enemies of God are those who threaten the existence of the Islamic community, those who persecute Muslims and, finally, polytheists. Islam and polytheism, which stands as the enemy of Muslims, cannot coexist. Pagans have to chose between faith or the sword. In reality, however, history has shown that, beside the Jews and the Christians, Islam has tolerated the presence of many other religious communities which have claimed to have a "book," when these fell under its domination and later when the Muslim troops reached the Ganges. Open, armed aggression against the polytheists ultimately seems to have been directed toward the hostility of narrow and barbaric paganism having no conception of a superior divinity. In practice, it was limited to the pagans of the Arabian Peninsula at the time of the Prophet.

The guarding of frontiers is a "holy war" by definition since its aim is to protect the Muslim community and to drive back enemy attacks. This particular form was of importance during the European counteroffensive.

Holy war against collective apostasy appears primarily as a scholastic, juridical exercise. Only one major historical example is known to us: the effort of a "prophet," Musailimah, immediately after the death of Muhammad, to gain the support of some of the recently Islamized tribes. Abu Bakr, the first successor, reestablished the unity of the peninsula. Collective apostasy is in fact secession. Muslim jurists agree in thinking that the treatment of the conquered should be of the severest type because they rejected the religion. The leader of the community, the imam, may call a *jihad* against groups of dissident believers. This is one of the most difficult and controversial aspects of Islamic doctrine. Islam asserts the believers' right on the basis of justice.

---

[74] *al-Jihad al-Akbar.*
[75] *Ribat.*
[76] *Baghi.*
[77] We are inspired in this above all by Khadduri, *War*, pp. 74 f.

26. .... Jihad: A Commitment to Universal Peace

Individuals who are victims of injustice arising out of real or imagined nonapplication of the Qur'ānic law enjoy the right to revolt. Moreover, the Qur'ān recommends that the Muslims remain a unified community. Violent contestations or dissidence should be checked. Between disorder and injustice, it appears that the doctrine gradually gravitated toward the second type of alternative. On a practical level, history shows that the Muslim armies were far more occupied with waging internal wars than with hostilities against the outside. Ultimately, it was the war of the conqueror which was "holy!"

The *jihad* against deserters and highway robbers corresponds to the traditional role assigned to armed forces of ensuring public security and internal law and order.

The holy war against monotheists is an awkward matter to describe since the image which was left of this institution, by history to a certain extent and by legal doctrine to a large extent, does not exactly coincide with the spirit of the Islamic revelation. Theoretically, the "People of the Book" who showed hostility toward Islam and the Muslims would have a choice of the following alternatives: faith, capitation tax, or war. This triple option is understandable only in reference to the basic Muslim conception of war and only by distinguishing between the individual and society. In reality, war is not waged against peoples but against states. At this level, Islam demands from authorities the possibility of openly spreading its religious message as well as freedom of conscience for such citizens who may wish to become Muslims. A refusal would lead to war. On the individual level, once military force has been imposed, Islam offers the option of adhering to the faith on payment of a personal and not a collective tax. Thus the ultimatum has to be made in this twofold perspective. If this is not the case, the war would be neither holy nor just since the Qru'ān itself formally forbids aggression and explicitly prohibits compulsion in religious matters.

Apart from the preceding conjectures, violence is forbidden and war is unjust. All believers participate in the "holy war," virtuous women and children included. On the other hand, only mature males who are independent and in good health participate in its military manifestation. Beyond loyalty and obedience toward his leader, the combatant must be motivated by good intentions. In this way he participates in a double holy war: on the battlefield where he presents himself in order to defend the cause of the religion and not in search of booty, and in the second coinciding form of *jihad* in his heart where he checks anger and greed so as to fight against his enemies with clemency and honesty.

Thus, in its widest sense, "holy war" does not mean active hostilities, even though antagonism between the Muslim community and the "world of war"

Effort... 27

is supposed to be permanent. If it assumes the form of active combat, the *jihad* would necessarily have to be a just war in its cause, its aim and in the manner in which it is waged. In the Qur'ān and prophetic tradition the references to the "holy war" in its broader meaning of effort are numerous. Classical Muslim literature does not cease to praise its merits. On the particular level of hostilities as such, the obligation is collective if Islam initiates the attack while individual if Muslim troops are engaged in the defense of the community. Holy war, therefore, can be both offensive and defensive.[78] When it is of a defensive nature, it presents no doctrinal problems since it corresponds to the essential right of self-preservation.

On the other hand, the aggressive *jihad* has been the subject of judicial and religious controversy, for neither the Qur'ān nor the prophetic tradition appear to prescribe it in any precise manner. Classical authors who wished to reconcile their points of view with the terms of the sacred law imagined a progressive succession of divine commandments. At first, patience and forgiveness were recommended to the Muslims after which they were allowed to fight against the aggressors. Then, in a third phase, the community was granted permission to initiate the combat at certain times of the year and, finally, to wage war without restrictions of time or place.[79] Even as an offensive operation, the "holy war" is supposed to remain a sanction against those who disobey God, opposing the establishment of the revealed law. To combat nonbelievers who prevent their fellows from embracing and following the paths of God became a meritorious virtue. This point of view qualifies the adjective "offensive."

Open hostility, as hostility in action, though it may be undeclared, makes it legitimate to use all means necessary for the defense of Islam. It is possible to imagine that the aim of the "holy war" is expressed in an alternate and opposing manner. In fact, does it aim more to subjugate than to convert the nonbelievers? Subjugating them should subsequently allow the population of conquered territories to freely choose the Islamic faith. The war would then be a sanction against governments which prevented the population from professing Islam. If, on the other hand, the main objective of violence was religious conversion, the holy war would then be punishment of nonbelief itself. Though this be a fundamental principle, the opinions of classical authors are divergent.[80] At the present time, the point of view of Muslim specialists is

---

[78] ibn-Taimiyyah, *On Public and Private Law*, pp. 135 f.
[79] Ghoneimi, *The Muslim Conception*, pp. 140 f.
[80] Abu Hanifah leans toward the first solution by fixing as a definition of the criteria of "domain of war" the security which the believers enjoy, whereas ash-Shafi'i advances the second idea which evidently gives a more aggressive aspect to the Islamic theory of international relations.

28................Jihad: A Commitment to Universal Peace

ialists is unanimous. On the one hand, it is not for man but for God alone to judge and punish disbelief. On the other hand, the theory of international relations could not be based on anything but Qur'ānic principles. Since compulsion in religious matters is formally forbidden, the aim of the war of force can therefore not be the conversion of non-Muslims.

When looking back at the events of the remote past, one can largely succeed in understanding how the usage of the "holy war" became distorted in Christian public opinion and also perhaps in the Islamic consciousness. By sacrificing himself for the defense of the religion and the cause of God, the believer was making the greatest and ultimate profession of his faith. He, the martyr, was promised the bliss of paradise. This religious zeal of the warriors doubtlessly stands as one of the reasons for the rapid geographical and political expansion of Islam. This, however, had never been one of the primary objectives of the holy war. Islam in no way seeks political dominion of the world or submission to the faith[81] but, on the contrary, condemns destruction and unnecessary violence. Since it aims at the harmony of the world and peace among men, it authorizes resorting to force in order to right evil and to curb iniquity. The prime objective of violence is not war as such, nor territorial expansion of the community, nor even religious proselytism, but the establishment of peace in justice.

The explanation for the rapidity of Islamic expansion can be found in political science. Conquests followed the traditional paths of migration and may be analyzed just like any historical phenomenon. The great strength of the warriors' faith provided them with a zeal and spirit which most certainly directly influenced their military victories and, indirectly, the subsequent Islamization of the conquered peoples. Thus, religion seems to have played no more than a purely psychological role in the conquest. The deformation of ideas can be explained by the coincidence of the two phenomena. However, the aggression and violence shown by the Muslim troops at times had no direct connection with the religious doctrine. One can gain some idea of the pure spirit of Islam by considering the manner in which the Prophet and his first successors treated the civil populations subjected to their rule in newly conquered territories. They were highly aware of the fact that they had no right other than the application of justice. Subsequently, however, if the political domination of the Muslim empire was spread mainly by arms, the Islamic faith was essentially spread by pacific ways. The fact that certain later Muslim leaders violated basic Qur'ānic rules in no way diminishes *jihad*'s divine and eternal value. This statement could seem incongruous in appearance,

---

[81]"If Allah would have willed, He would have made you one community," an-Nahl: 93 (Blachère).

especially since Muslim law – which is normative and idealized – is not the result of a codification of existing practices. It nevertheless shows that one should practice great caution in analyzing historical facts and events which contradict the Qur'ānic revelation.

There are two mental attitudes – the one objective and the other subjective – which deserve mention, for they also contributed to the degradation of the concept of the "holy war." Islam had hardly attained stability when it appeared as the torch of civilization, being permeated with basic Qur'ānic moral principles and benefiting from the refined culture of certain conquered peoples. The believers were most probably tempted to transmit their ideology to the neighboring populations crushed by the despotic feudal system and oppressed by the tyranny of ecclesiastic hierarchies. History repeats itself. The example of aggression undertaken in order to "liberate" peoples from injustice and servitude is not unique! Moreover, the fact that the Qur'ān forbids aggression as well as opening hostilities without valid reasons was to encourage Muslim leaders to enumerate the reasons for the just war which they were waging. The procedure soon gave the conflicts the character of reciprocity. The religious element of the Muslim holy war asserted itself especially during the European counterattacks of the tenth and eleventh centuries which hid behind Christianity to reconquer Spain and brandished the sword so as to reclaim the holy places of Palestine. For both Christianity and Islam, respect for religion served as a pretext and motivation for a war of conquest.

As a result of the confrontation between Christianity and Islam, there remained only a somewhat truncated version of the concept of holy war, retaining only a specifically military characteristic. In the West, as much as in the Muslim world (if not more so), political and religious matters were inextricably linked at that time. The Christian in those days sought his salvation in his struggle against the Muslim. Even before the sword of the Crusades, the sovereign-pontiff Alexander II in 1063 granted the absolution of sins to believers fighting to expel the Muslims from the Iberian Peninsula. Islam, like Christianity, offered eternal salvation for all soldiers who fell in the "holy war." It is possible to establish certain illustrative similarities between the two religions as a result of their first great political confrontation from the eleventh century in spite of the tragic, bloody events which took place all over, as well as of the periods of understanding and near-fraternity which existed for some time.

On the individual level, the crusader set out to massacre the nonbeliever upon the oftentimes repeated call of Urbain II: "God wills it." As to the Muslim warrior, his was the moral obligation of being motivated by good intentions and to be in a state of "greater holy war," – that is, of restraining his anger and passion in order to treat his enemy magnanimously. Moreover, Islam had an institutional safeguard for the monotheistic minorities which had

30.....................Jihad: A Commitment to Universal Peace

come under its political control. In general, these minorities suffered no particular persecution. On the other hand, the Spanish "Reconquest" ended in none other than the expulsion of the last "Moriscos" from the Iberian Peninsula. They were largely autochthons descended from converts.

In Palestine, the crusader kings rallied the Christians of the Levant into one state, without attempting to organize a special institution for the Muslim minorities nor even giving any thought to a true coexistence. Finally, on the judicial level, the Qur'ān safeguards the clergy,[82] declaring that God protects non-Muslim places of worship: "Did not God check one set of people by means of another, there would surely have been pulled down monasteries, churches, synagogues, and mosques, in which the name of God is commemorated in abundant measure."[83] This prohibition is corroborated and elucidated by the prophetic tradition which forbids soldiers to do harm to any religious persons, whereas they could logically have been the primary targets if the motive of the "holy war" had been religious. Without putting Western civilization on trial, we should nevertheless mention by way of contrast that several centuries later, the founders of international law in Europe excluded the Muslim "infidels" from the benefits of the law of wars. Yet, the concept of "holy war" remains branded as the expression of the Muslims' religious fanaticism. How ineradicable are the prejudices!

Islam is the return to primordial unity. All effort, violence, and war are necessary to combat those who, by opposing divine plans, are hostile to justice and peace. The enemy is disorder, disharmony, and evil in all its forms. Man carries these elements in himself; they are all his tendencies and temptations which oppose his personal unity. By becoming interiorized, the holy war sought to encourage the Muslim to wage a constant battle against himself, against the inertia and distortions of his cultural and social milieu, thereby preparing himself for "the task of material, intellectual, and moral regeneration which justifies the efficient demand for a better earthly existence"[84] for him, his community, and all of mankind. Through his personal struggle, the believer declares his quality of manhood and, by simultaneously taming his selfishness and restraining his passions, he asserts the rights and duties of all individuals living in a society governed by order and righteousness.

The holy war is permanent, without interruption or end. The Muslims are convinced of this. The Qur'ān explicitly indicates it: "And strive in His cause as you ought to strive (with sincerity and under discipline). He has chosen

---

[82]al-Baqarah: 191.
[83]al-Hajj: 40 (Masson).
[84]Abdel Jalil, *Aspects*, p. 75.

Violence. 31

you...It is He Who has named you Muslims."[85] Good is in constant conflict with evil; such is the will of God. The world of Islam, understood as the reign of unity and equilibrium, is in constant confrontation with the world of war which is considered as disorder and excess. The believer is obliged to take part in the *jihad*, both in its inner moral expression as in its concrete, visceral manifestation. The specifically military aspect of the "holy war" is, however, secondary and intermittent. The paths leading to the total Islamization of the world are numerous. They do not stem from the wish of the believers but rather from the divine will.[86] In all eternity, there is only one true reality: the existence of God alone. The Qur'ān does not bring a new message to humanity. It affirms itself as the continuation and culminating fruit of the monotheistic revelation. All men are free to embrace the faith; the believer would be lacking in humility and would consequently be disobeying God if he attempted to impose his faith by force. If his convictions make him pugnacious, his respect for the law restrains his zeal. Thus, the holy war is "surpassed and transfigured by peace in God, by consciousness of the absolute."[87]

The notion of holy war is always topical in Islam. The Prophet after all said: "*Jihad* will last until the Day of Judgment." This is obvious, for in human society there will always be progress to be made, injustice to combat, and oppression to abolish. If the contemporary Muslim world participates – albeit in scattered groups – in the life of international society, one should not see this only as a reconciliation between the "Dar al-Islam" and the "Dar al-Harb."[88] Good and evil cannot be reconciled; order and injustice cannot coexist. On the contrary, it could be first and foremost a case of a certain transformation in the "world of war." In reality, the Islamic states as such are no longer threatened because of their religious doctrine, and all things considered, rare indeed are those Muslims who are persecuted because they proclaim "Our Lord is Allah." The military expression of the holy war would thus no longer have any reason to exist. The *jihad* of the heart, tongue, and hand remain necessary for the preservation of Islam's humanitarian values, and are indispensable for the task of the social and economic development of the Muslim world. The allegory of armed effort, magnified by Muslim literature, will most certainly persist but will be taken in its strictly literal sense. As a matter of fact, the sword "above all symbolizes the power of the word, a thing which should moreover be rather self-evident, especially since it is one of the meanings generally attributed to the sword, and which is not

---

[85] al-Hajj: 78 (Masson).
[86] Yunus: 99-100 and al-Kahf: 29.
[87] Schuon, *Comprendre*, p. 69.
[88] As well as Khadduri's claim in the epilogue to *War*, pp. 268 f.

32..................Jihad: A Commitment to Universal Peace

foreign to Christianity either."[89]

Violence

Violence is permanent and inevitable. All kinds of antagonism have increasingly torn the world apart ever since God created man. Islam's sociological doctrine[90] sees several reasons for this. It resides as much in human nature – the tendency toward aggression, love of power and fortune, jealousy and rivalry of interests – as in the makeup of society: contestation and defense of central authority. Nevertheless, truth must triumph over error, good must vanquish evil, and justice crush injustice. Antagonism between individuals, groups, and nations is unavoidable: "If your Lord had so willed, He could have made mankind one people: but they will not cease to dispute."[91] God explicitly indicates that human beings "are enemies to each other."[92] Here, it is interesting to be reminded of the fact that, if the fall of Adam bore no consequences for the intrinsic nature of man, it did have a consequence for the mechanism of social relations. War not only represents an inevitability but also a fundamental necessity for the harmonization of the world, by means of mutually neutralizing men.[93]

More than being legalistic in essence, Islam is a revelation which resolutely comprehends the objectivity of facts. The believer is "passive" if he is open to and in submission to the divine decree, but he is consequently called to resist evil – even by violence – so as to participate in upholding the true foundation of humanity: justice. The passive charity which Christian doctrine recommends to one who has been slapped on the cheek shocks Muslim reasoning, which considers it unrealistic and illogical because it is unnatural. The enemy is essentially he who practices evil and enforces injustice. He is, for the same reason, the enemy of God and His law. He cannot reasonably expect true "love" from the believer. The latter is moreover not permitted to "love" an enemy who hates God.[94]

This dynamism of faith, upheld by the conviction of possessing the revealed truth, has left a permanent mark on the Muslim's conception of human

---

[89] See, for instance, Guénon, "Sayful-Islam," who recalls in this regard, more specifically on p. 59, that Christ himself had declared: "I have not come to you bearing peace but the sword," Matthew 10:34.
[90] See, in particular, ibn-Khaldoun, *Mouqaddima*.
[91] Hūd: 118 (Blachère).
[92] al-A'raf: 24.
[93] "... If God did not check one set of people by another, the earth would indeed be full of mischief. But God is full of bounty to all the worlds," al-Baqarah: 251 (Masson).
[94] Galwash, *The Religion*, pp. 108 f.

Violence 33

relations and has equally determined, to a very large extent, the rules of war. Pointless mercy or passive compassion shown to an evil man represents an injustice with regard to the community, a threat to its security, and an infringement on divine will. It is thus that Islam "strikes us with the unbending nature of its convictions and also by the pugnacity of its faith; these two complementing aspects, the one interior and static, the other external and dynamic, essentially stem from a consciousness of the absolute which, on the one hand, makes us impervious to doubt and, on the other, rejects error with violence."[95]

History shows us that no divine or ideological revelation claiming to regulate earthly matters has been able to express itself in an entirely pacific manner since it had to assert itself against the violent reaction of the sociological milieu which it aimed to reform. Urged on by their divine mission, God's various prophets had to resort to violence which legitimized war, simultaneously giving it a character of legitimate defense. The very manner in which they conducted their battles provides an illustrative example of the way man has to struggle in order to let good triumph.[96]

From these examples, and in particular from that of the Prophet Muhammad, we can distinguish three specific characteristics which gives us a better grasp of the Muslim understanding of foreign relations. These three elements – piety, pugnacity, and magnanimity[97] – could at first appear contradictory. In the Islamic perspective they are complementary. Piety is submission to God and unshakable attachment to His law. The combative spirit resides in love of justice, respect for the truth, and a "passionate zeal for the cause of God." Finally, magnanimity, which is not devoid of a certain implacability toward traitors, is a reminder of divine mercy toward man. If nonbelief appears essentially as injustice, the revelation is a mercy and faith a grace.

Thus, it is beyond doubt that in Islam there exists a doctrinal element which is eminently combative and a historical tradition of war. However, violence, taken in its broader meaning, is a legitimate function of justice. "Be it a question of exterior and social order or internal and spiritual order, war should always make an equal attempt at establishing harmony and stability...This is the same as saying that its normal resolution – which is definitely its only justification – is peace."[98] Thus, we find a definition of the *jihad* in the sense implied in the Muslim tradition. Islam not only preached toler-

---

[95]Schuon, *Comprendre*, p. 49.
[96]Abu Zahra, *La conception*, p. 13 f.
[97]Schuon, *Comprendre*, pp. 177-118.
[98]Guenon, "Sayful-Islam," p. 59.

ance but gave it the force of law.[99] Proselytism, no matter how zealous and sincere it may be, could not effectively be implemented by force since it would contradict divine plans, being an expression of human arrogance.

The verse forbidding compulsion in religious matters seems to have been revealed in Medinah, at the very moment when the Muslim community had been strongly structured and no longer needed to fear its direct enemies[100] since it had become the main military force of the Arabian Peninsula. This chronological precision assumes a certain importance since it explains and justifies *a priori* certain reactions of the Islamic community. The prohibition of religious compulsion not only protects nonbelievers from excessive proselytic zeal on the part of the Muslims but, more importantly, it also attempts to counteract any compulsion or persecution which would affect certain loyal subjects – potential believers – whether isolated or within Muslim community. It is also in this sense that the divine injunction should be understood. The Muslim community placed its power at the service of those of its adherents who suffered because of their faith.

Being fundamentally realistic, the Qur'ānic revelation admits violence and legalizes war. However, battle is permitted only to check injustice. The permission to engage in armed combat has explicit motives and is immediately limited. War must necessarily be declared as a form of self-protection or legitimate defense; hostilities must be waged with decency and according to divine ways. Aggression and the initiation of combat without any valid reasons are forbidden: "Fight in the cause of God those who fight you, but do not transgress limits, for God loves not transgressors."[101] Violence is answered by violence, injustice by force.

Other than the defense of the community, injustice and persecution are also valid reasons for authorizing war: "To those against whom war is made, permission is given [to fight] because they are wronged; and verily, God is most powerful for their aid; [they are] those who have been expelled from their homes in defiance of right [for no cause] except that they say, 'Our Lord is God.'"[102] The oppression or exile to which isolated believers in minority groups living outside the Muslim world often fall victim represents a "casus belli" through a sociological or communal assimilation which can be easily understood if one refers to the Muslim conception of the "collective man."

---

[99]"There is no compulsion in religion! The true way distinguishes itself from error," al-Baqarah: 256 (Masson).
[100]Bêchebichy, *Les relations*, p. 18.
[101]al-Baqarah: 190 (Blachère) as well as al-Baqarah: 194.
[102]al-Hajj: 39-40. (Reda).

Violence...35

The formulation of permission itself is full of reservations inasmuch as it poses conditions which are difficult to express. Legal permission can become a moral obligation for the community and for the believers individually, if the facts appear clear and evident. In effect, they may not refrain from intervening in order to put an end to injustice and to reestablish order according to divine plans. This is even more so in the case of persecution of a believer: "And turn them out from where they have turned you out, for tumult and oppression are worse than slaughter."[103] Islam stands to defend not only the Muslims but also persecuted Jews and Christians. This kind of armed intervention characteristically corresponds to what nineteenth-century European international law meant by "humanitarian intervention." This is a literal case of the assertion of basic human rights: security, guarantee of man's person and property, respect for freedom of thought. Islam's military power was the background and guarantee of this assertion.

Ligitimate causes of war are the defense of the community and protection of the oppressed on a general level. The doctrine more precisely defined the various motives which entrusted believers with the authority to take up arms: to safeguard the Muslim faith; to defend, maintain, and consolidate the Islamic community; to counter any plots which seek to turn the believers away from their religion; to guard what is recognized by divine and human laws; to protect one's own person; to right an injustice committed toward one's brothers in religion as well as to monotheists who have paid their capitation taxes. However, man's natural tendencies toward violence, his greed for domination, desire for revenge, material motivation or tendencies of pillage are all considered as malevolent and iniquitous causes. In short, aggression is forbidden.

In practice, the concept of "aggression" is eminently subjective and difficult to define. It would perhaps be useful to give it a psychological meaning: the provocation or triggering of hostilities which aim at dominating or at imposing a certain concept of the world or to steal land and possessions. Inasmuch as it can be defined, the intention plays a determining role. Sometimes it is brash and sometimes discrete, good or bad. It may conceal legitimate aspirations or, on the contrary, acts of violence. Nonetheless, the Qur'ānic prohibition is precise and absolute, having a bearing on all possibilities, since it is not only legal but also religious. Neither the believer nor the community can hide their true intentions or their intimate desires from God Who "knows and hears all."

---

[103]al-Baqarah: 191 (Blachère). This verse permits, in other respects, a better understanding of certain human and psychological aspects of the conflict which since 1948 has torn the Arab and Islamic Middle East.

36. . . . . Jihad: A Commitment to Universal Peace

Islamic literature takes pleasure in recalling and explaining the decisions Prophet Muhammad made when he was leading the growing Muslim community. It is not important whether or not the traditions which are reported seem exaggerated or even fictitious to *certain* critics. The fact that they vividly influence the contemporary Muslim conscience represents the "furtive anticipation of an ideal order"[104] which, when projected, illustrates the conviction of the believers and becomes part of a vision for the future. It would probably not be superfluous to devote some attention to it.

Necessity soon forced the Prophet to organize an army to repel enemy attacks and to dispatch preventive expeditions against hostile neighbors. A man of integrity, a fine politician and brilliant strategist, Muhammad felt the need to "dissuade" the enemies of his community. He had to counter attacks of pillage; he had to ensure peace and tranquility on the caravan routes. Finally, in the context of tribal wars which were tearing the Arabian Peninsula apart at that time, armed forces proved to be of vital necessity in order not to encourage "the enemies of Islam or to endanger the very existence of the state, which was in the first stages of its evolution."[105] Thus the battles, even those initiated by the Prophet, assumed the character of a response to provocation or that of self-protective measures.

The argument is likely. Threatened by the Makkans who feared for the unity and supremacy of their city, by the Jews who refused to see in Muhammad the prophet foretold and who were struggling to preserve the economic importance they enjoyed in Medinah, denigrated by the Christians who raised their cries of impostor, and challenged from the inside by certain inhabitants of Medinah (accused of being "hypocrites" by the Qur'ān), the developing community truly seemed to be in danger. The opposition of established neighboring societies was violent toward both the Islamic community and converts, isolated Muslims who, by their adhering to the faith, had broken the ties of tribal solidarity and protection. These historical considerations and sociological conclusions justify those arguments claiming that the Prophet was obliged to use arms for legitimate defense.

For Muslim literature, the battles fought by the Prophet illustrate the particular nature of Islamic war: it is just in its causes, defensive in its initiative, decent in its proceedings, pacific in its end, and humanitarian in its treatment of the conquered enemy. The manner in which Muhammad waged battles is

---

[104]Abdallah Laroui, *L'idéologie arabe contemporaine* (Paris: Maspero, 1967), p. 103. After this: Laroui, *L'idéologie arabe*.
[105]Esade F. Tugay, *Mahomet, le Prophète d'Allah* (Cairo: Eastern Press, 1951), p. 276. After this: Tugay, *Mahomet*.

Violence. 37

of primary juridical importance and still theoretically valid in our time. Recourse to violence is dependent on and made legitimate by the adversary's attitude. The immense magnanimity shown by the Prophet ought to prove that even the battles which he initiated were of a preventive character. The prophetic traditions show this clearly. For example, even before besieging Makkah, when it was yet uncertain as to whether weapons would be issued, upon hearing one of his army leaders singing "today is the day when blood will flow, we will have no pity," Muhammad snatched the banner indicating his military authority from his hands. He then gave it to another soldier well-known for his peace-loving nature, expressly ordering the troops not to revert to arms unless they were attacked.

The expulsion of the Jewish tribes of Medinah, an often-mentioned fact, illustrates the sometimes implacable nature of Muhammad. For Muslim authors this was an indispensable act of legitimate defense. By reconstructing the facts such as Islamic sources tell them to us, we can explain the violent nature of the measure taken with regard to the Jews. Their dogmatic hostility was vehement and bitingly sarcastic. Their great economic importance as well as their cultural superiority over the Medinans gave them considerable influence. Muhammad, who at first offered them the possibility of assimilating themselves into the community of believers as an autonomous entity, was very soon obliged to abandon the hope of converting them or of making reliable allies of them. Ever ready to plot and join forces with the enemies of the Muslims, they were all the more fearsome in that they possessed fortified positions right within the Islamic territory. Faced with the "insolubility" of Judaism,[106] and for the very safety of the community, Muhammad decided to eliminate this force.

Two of the three tribes accused of high treason were expelled and permitted to take their personal estate with them: the one (Bani Nadhir) for having attempted to murder the Prophet; the other (Bani Qainuqa') for having spied for the enemy. As for the third tribe (Bani Qureiza), they had broken an agreement made with the Muslims by trying to rally the neighboring tribes with a view to making a communal attack on Medinah which was besieged at that time. For two weeks the Muslims besieged their fortress, forcing them to surrender. The men were court-martialed while the women and children were put into slavery. On the level of dogma and jurisdiction, the elimination of the Jewish tribes does not in the Muslim doctrine have any particular importance since this was a question of legitimate defense; treason is moreover punish-

---

[106] Edmond Rabbath, "Pour une théorie du droit international musulman," *Egyptian Journal of International Law* (1950):13. After this: Rabbath, "Pour une théorie."

38 . . . . Jihad: A Commitment to Universal Peace

able by death in all known systems of law. Furthermore, the tragic massacre of the men of the Bani Qureiza was not a sanction of the Islamic canon. In actual fact, the Jews under attack requested that an old Arab, known for his wisdom and justice, decide their fate in accordance with Hebrew law. It was the application of the Jewish law which led to the inhuman harshness of this decision.[107]

There is no real need to quote any further examples of the Prophet's behavior, even though they abound in the prophetic tradition. On the other hand, two particular aspects of the doctrine which are of a certain topical importance should be mentioned: the claim to protect isolated believers in the "world of war" and the theoretical attitude toward "internal wars."

It is on the level of protecting isolated believers that the defensive value of Muslim violence is both the most logical and debatable. The argument of intervention for the protection of persecuted Muslim minorities can at first seem to permit all sorts of excesses in practice. We need only to remember the specifically Muslim conception of "collective man" according to which all believers, subject to the divine law, are grouped into one homogenous entity. Oppression imposed upon any one of them represents an attack against the entire community. Furthermore, on a sociological level, the great initial "revolution" of Islam aimed at replacing tribal or blood relations and loyalties in Arabia with a religious bond. By embracing Islam, the individual once again excluded himself from established society, voluntarily placing himself "out of the law." Since he was thus "detribalized," he no longer enjoyed any protection and ran the risk of becoming the victim of the worst arbitrariness, no longer having the preventive guarantee of blood revenge.

The Islamic community had to immediately assert itself as the protector of the Muslims. The assertion of its power and of its protective role assumed a growing importance with the adherence or support of an increasing number of individuals. By extension, attacks on the community were not only intended as persecution of isolated believers but also as a prohibition for individuals to embrace Islam if they so wished. It is in this context that the proselytizing aspect of the religion appears, and it is here that the verse forbidding religious compulsion assumes its fullest meaning. It is indeed "important for one who preaches a sublime cause aiming at defending faith and individual freedom, that mankind be aware of this cause, that each man should have the right to freely choose from among the different doctrines the one which most suits him and is in greatest accord with reason. If a king

---

[107]Tradition reports that Sa'd ibn-Mu'adh, prince of the tribe of Aws, referred to Deuteronomy 20: 10-15, for its "Law of Anathema."

Violence. 39

or despot oppresses his people, restricting their freedom and preventing the truth from reaching them, the apostle has the right to smash the barrier which surges up between these oppressed people and his message."[108] Constraint and prohibition of free choice in religion are the very stigma borne by the world of injustice and strife. In this respect, the Qur'ān's attitude is very clear since it does not admit intervention in a non-Muslim country which is tied to the world of Islam by treaty: "But if they seek your aid in religion, it is your duty to help them, except against a people with whom you have a treaty of mutual alliance."[109] Islam committed itself to not threatening non-Muslim communities or imposing its faith upon them, on the condition that they did not persecute their citizens who had accepted the Qur'ānic revelation and acknowledged the veracity of Muhammad's mission.[110]

Classical doctrine is scanty in its indications on the second aspect under consideration in this chapter: the ordering of inter-Islamic relations. This is understandable since the legal doctrine of Islam was constructed upon the myth of a homogeneous community, all believers forming one "nation." Very early on, however, under the pressure of circumstances, the theory of political unity was debated. Muhammad's settling in Medinah put an immediate end to the permanent hostilities which divided the city's two main tribes. However, even before the death of the Prophet, an attempted revolt divided Arabia. Abu Bakr checked it. The more authority and obedience the community leader commanded, the more this idea took root. Ibn Khaldun even goes to the point of considering as just and holy any war waged to confirm central power.[111] Quoting order and justice as their motive and invariably invoking Islamic principles, Muslim factions confronted one another in bloody battles, each party claiming to be waging a just and holy war and at the same time accusing the adversary of condemnable hostilities.

Since resorting to violence is authorized for the defense of the community and for the elimination of injustice, these possibilities can sometimes seem paradoxical in light of the fact that community authority was identified with the caliphate. Injustice is not the exclusive invention of the outside world. Islamic unity was destroyed by religious schisms or, more simply, by political

---

[108] Abu Zahra, *La conception*, p. 22.
[109] al-Anfal: 72 (Blachère).
[110] The first treaties signed by the Prophet explicitly mention it. The accord signed with the Christians of Najran stipulated: "They will not be oppressed as long as they do not oppress anyone." See also the letter of Muhammad to Emperor Heraclius, reproduced by Hamidullah in his *Muslim Conduct*, p. 170.
[111] "The Hand of God is extended upon the community and the one who separates himself falls into the fire," says the Prophet. Notice that the "community" is understood here as the collectivity which implicitly follows all the Qur'ānic principles.

40. . . . . Jihad: A Commitment to Universal Peace

ambitions which were often based on the quest for local or cultural identity. On the legal level, this matter was of great importance since it plainly addressed the problem of the fusion of the spiritual and secular spheres. However, anathema and excommunication were not characteristic in Islam's religious history. The distinction between orthodoxy and heresy was steeped with mutual tolerance. Since the eleventh and twelvth century, under the influence of Imam al-Ghazzali, Muslim doctrine rejected confession, declaring that acknowledgment of men as believers depended solely on their accepting the basic articles of faith. Dynastic differences, even though it was the rejection of Sunni caliphal authority, were not supposed to constitute a reason for exclusion.[112]

Jurists therefore arrived at the point of considering the possibility of "subnationalities," depending on the power they exercised and on the administration and jurisdiction they applied. In this connection, the prophetic traditions give additional elements. In the messages he sent them, Muhammad assured the foreign princes that he would leave their power intact if they embraced Islam.[113] The Qur'ān also admits the division of believers into various political entities, recommending that Muslims give just aid if needs be: "If two parties among the believers fall into a quarrel, make peace between them, but if one of them transgresses beyond bounds against the other, then fight against the one that transgresses until it complies with the command of God. But if it complies, then make peace between them with justice and be fair, for God loves those who are fair [and just]."[114]

In the context of "rules of war," there are terms concerning armed conflicts between opposing Muslim entities. As a matter of fact, the stipulations of classical doctrine appear admirably "modern." They do of course envisage dissidence – "civil wars" – rather than interstate battles. Rebels enjoy *de facto* recognition of their government: their jurisdiction over the territory they command is considered legal and valid for as long as they retain their authority. Neither the leaders nor partisans of the dissident group are responsible or impeachable for the human or material losses caused by the battle.[115] Concern-

---

[112]Ignaz Goldziher, *Le dogme et la loi de l'Islam: Histoire du développement dogmatique et juridique de la religion musulmane*, translated by Félix Arin (Paris: Geuthner, 1958), p. 154. After this: Goldziher, *Le dogme*.

[113]Hamidullah, *Muslim Conduct*, who cites, in other respects, on pp. 266 f., various examples, of which Bahrain and Oman are two.

[114]al-Hujurat: 9 (Reda). One can also see an allusion to the possibility of inter-Muslim wars in an-Nisa': 92: "... If the deceased was part of a group hostile to you and he was a believer ..." (Blachère).

[115]Majid Khadduri, *The Islamic Law of Nations*, Shaybani "Siyar" (Baltimore: Johns Hopkins, 1966), pp. 218-219. After this: Khadduri, *The Islamic Law*.

Magnanimity... 41

ing the waging of hostilities, the laws are identical to those governing war with outside enemies, with two favorable exceptions: prisoners cannot be put to death, and property cannot be seized and distributed as booty.

The division of the community was accepted by force of circumstance. However, the doctrine contains few precise legal terms relevant to relationships between Islamic countries or to the treatment of nationals of one Muslim country who chose to live in another Muslim country.[116] The fact that events have not exerted a great influence on legal doctrine can be understood in the general perspective of Muslim law and by historical analysis. In truth, "internal" conflicts which led to the community's becoming fragmented assumed a particular character which defies initial analysis. In contrast to the wars which followed the fall of the Roman Empire and which took place in the eleventh and twelfth centuries in Europe, these conflicts were never motivated by "nationalistic" feelings. It was rather a matter of various *coup d'états* which established new dynasties or divided the Muslim world into an infinite number of small states or autonomous principalities. These political upheavals generally took place without excessive violence and did not have long-lasting harmful consequences for civilian populations. At the same time, no significant breakdown came about in the general political system nor in the cultural unity. The absence of nationalism and the fundamentally Muslim psychological attitude of attachment to the leader rather than to abstract theories or ideologies explain why Islamic "international law" – as opposed to what happened in the Christian West – was concerned with defining and governing relations with territories not under Qur'ānic jurisdiction and not with internal relations in the "world of Islam."

At the conclusion of this discussion dealing with the concept of war in Islam, a final remark is necessary. It would be historically incorrect to claim that none of the wars undertaken by the Muslims were motivated by a spirit of aggression or greed, but this aggressiveness could not be blamed on the religion, regardless of the violence of certain Qur'ānic verses calling for war against the invaders. Legitimate defense was of course not the only reason for the wars which the Muslims began. The desire to dominate, the spirit of aggression, and the attraction of booty were certainly not always absent. The historical explanation of these conflicts is more a matter of political science or sociology than of law. An objective analysis of the doctrine clearly shows that force was not a primordial element of Islamic expansion. The Western

---

[116]Hamidullah, *Muslim Conduct*, pp. 128 f., cites the example of Saladin who bestowed a pension, purse, and self-jurisdiction upon the North African students living in Cairo.
[117]Miguel Palacios, "contacts de la spiritualité musulmane et de la spiritualité chrétienne," in *L'Islam et L'Occident*, Paris (Cohiers du Sud), p. 69.

42. . . . . Jihad: A Commitment to Universal Peace

bias which attributes the rapid expansion of Islam to the sword "should be rejected or reduced to a role of at most a secondary importance which aided and made possible the success of many other factors of a spiritual nature. Without these, the brutal force of the holy wars would have been fruitless."[117] The very fact that the subjugated peoples subsequently rejected Arab rule but retained the Muslim faith constitutes a formal proof.

Magnanimity

The waging of war, both throughout the history of wars as well as in our day and age, is greatly determined by the aim of the belligerent party. The very definition of the conflict unfortunately too often proves to be more important than existing international legislation or generally accepted moral laws. It is impossible to find an all-inclusive definition, whether historical or cultural. Violence can suddenly surge up as a necessity in relation to the image a group has of man and society, of their reciprocal roles or of their mutual relations. Islam has developed an original conception of the world, society, and the individual. The aim of war is strictly defined and determines both the manner of waging battle as well as the appropriate manner of dealing with the enemy.

In the Islamic doctrine, even if war sometimes represents the negation of compassion, it may not in any way stand against virtue and justice since God authorized combat under specific circumstances of legitimate defense. The fact that Muhammad and the prophets who preceded him had to resort to arms proves that violence is legitimate and that it can be committed in such a way as to respect elementary humanitarian laws.[118] The Muslim soldier would thus be guided by the Qur'ānic principles and the example of the Prophet. He would be able to respect the humanity of the enemy since it is not peoples but soldiers who struggle against each other in war. Humanity and bloodbath, justice and violence have to exist side by side on the battlefield.

At the same time, it is impossible to understand the Muslim philosophy which reconciles armed combat and compassion without referring to what at a very early stage proved to be the spiritual climate of Islam. It is also necessary, in this connection, to consider the particular expression of the religion as Muhammad incarnates it for the Muslims. Piety, which first and foremost means submission to the absolute, forces man into humility and, consequently, to generosity. The Qur'ān and Muslim doctrine often associate effort and struggle with patience, generosity, and forgiveness.[119] Humility, re-

---

[118]Abu Zahra, *La conception*, p. 11.
[119]ibn-Taimiyyah, *On Public and Private Law*, pp. 150 f., for example.

Magnanimity..43

sulting from an innate sense of the unseen world, compensates for aggressiveness in the manifestation of power. Piety clears the way for combativity — it is the affirmation of truth by force, and if needs be, by combative force. It is the struggle and effort made against oneself in relation to the world in order to make the divine word apparent. Combative force is always implacable toward those who consciously oppose truth (tyrants and traitors) and foreshadows divine justice. Thus, it cannot be vindictive and, even less, cruel. Thus, piety, which brings about combat, tempers the latter so that the two ways continue to culminate in magnanimity.[120]

Legal doctrine and popular belief are correct in emphasizing the extraordinary magnanimity displayed by Muhammad during the various battles he fought. This beneficence is admirable, not only in the light of the customs of that time, but also by comparison with the actions of the preceding prophets as recorded in the Bible.[121] On the level of doctrine, the requirement that warriors show compassion is expressed in two ways. First of all, the combatant is supposed to go into action motivated by good intentions – that is, he should want to defend the religion and not go in search of booty. Second, with regard to the battle itself, he must apply both forms of the "holy war" which the religion enjoins: the "greater *jihad*," the spiritual battle which compels him to bridle his anger and (baser) instincts and the struggle against the enemy of justice. The validity of the cause in no way implies that the enemy may be annihilated. On the contrary, the war is ever-just on the condition that the battle be waged in a manner imbued with compassion, no matter what the actions of the foe may be.

"O you who believe! Stand up firmly for God, as witnesses to fair dealing, and let not the hatred of others to you make you swerve to wrong and depart from justice."[122] This verse defines and sums up the entire Islamic ruling concerning the manner of waging war. Neither the commander of the army nor the isolated soldier may ignore the humanitarian rules imposed by the Qur'ānic revelation. As a whole, the terms of this revelation seek to define the enemy; to stipulate the formalities which precede the opening of armed conflict; to determine what treatment is given to the vanquished prisoners, be

---

[120]See concerning the explanation of Schuon, *Comprendre*, pp. 117-124.

[121]It is interesting to note on this that the Islamic doctrine rejects the authenticity of acts of useless violence and the cruelty of the Jewish prophets. The Muslims believe, in fact, that the transmission of it is in error and that all the messengers of God who preceded Muhammad and who had been obligated to resort to arms in order to affirm the truth had conducted their hostilities on the basis of humanity, never going beyond the limits imposed by the truth. See Abu Zahra, *La conception*, pp. 14-15.

[122]al-Ma'idah: 8 (Blachère). In verse 2 of the same sura, the Qur'ān warns that hatred does not lead the believers to "an abuse of law."

44. .Jihad: A Commitment to Universal Peace

they soldiers or civilians; and to divide up the war booty. The legal doctrine provides numerous rules which, for the most part, are of a distinctly humanitarian nature: prohibition of inflicting unnecessary suffering, prohibition of excess, protection of personal property and estate. These minutely detailed stipulations are presented in the form of specific examples which are nevertheless sufficiently concordant so as to allow for the establishment of general principles. With the exception of a few noteworthy examples,[123] the rules governing the waging of battles are disseminated in works of science, general jurisprudence, philosophy, history, literature, religious exegesis, or else in works dealing with the military, art, political morality, fiscal treatises, diplomacy, or expeditions.[124]

The established rules covered the whole war process, from the beginning to the end of hostilities. They draw their obligating power from the "fear of God." The prophetic traditions report that "every time the Messenger of God sent an army or a detachment ahead, he personally advised the commander to fear God Almighty and ordered the accompanying Muslims to perform good deeds, that is, to behave with decency."[125] The cornerstone of the entire structure resides in the prohibition of excess. This is at the base of all ethical and legal philosophies of Islam. The instructions of the Prophet, as well as those of his successors, emphasized the necessity for the Muslim soldiers to abstain from needlessly shedding blood or from destroying properties as long as military realities did not call for such actions. Muslim jurists seem to be perfectly aware of having made innovations in the domain of laws pertaining to war.[126]

The prohibition of excess is the very postulation of modern war law. However, since war is considered a sanction in Islamic judicial doctrine, the law of retaliation should be applied. This reciprocity is nevertheless strictly limited by certain elementary humanitarian values. Retaliation had been immediately tempered in Islam, on a general level, by the exhortation to be compassionate and patient.[127] In any event, recourse to retaliation is specifically conditioned by the prohibition of going beyond the bounds of human-

---

[123]Shaybani, for example.
[124]*Ghazawat*. See Rabbath, "Pour une théorie," pp. 9-10. We note, in passing, that the practice of the Muslim leaders, apart from those of the other orthodox successors of the Prophet, did not rest upon legal authority. The importance of precedents which were at times created must not be totally ignored. Hamidullah, *Muslim Conduct*, p. 24.
[125]Khadduri, *The Islamic Law*, pp. 75-76.
[126]Khadduri, *The Islamic Law*, p. 92.
[127]ash-Shura: 43, which recommends mercy and patience. Verse 40 deals with pardon. In fact, the entire passage of this sura merits being cited (36-43), for it eloquently demonstrates the fundamentally peaceful spirit of Islam, in times of war as well as in times of peace.

Magnanimity..45

ity.[128] Moreover, the law of retaliation would not be applicable if it were to bring about the violation of a Qur'ānic instruction.[129] Understood in this light, it prevents the Muslim combatant from resorting to excessive reprisals because of a narrow spirit of reciprocity which takes on the form of revenge.

Islam has minutely elaborated laws pertaining to the manner of waging war. We shall limit ourselves to simply emphasizing them here and shall return to some specific considerations later.

Hostilities must always be preceded by a declaration[130] or an ultimatum so that the enemy is not taken by surprise. Moreover, in an effort to reduce the consequences of combat, Muslim law limits them to strictly military aims, and clearly distinguishes between combatants and noncombatants. By extension, it prohibits needless destruction and the use of arms causing far-reaching destruction,[131] as well as any other indiscriminate measures, such as poisoning food sources or water supplies for such actions would affect civilians not taking part in combat.[132] Ignominious procedures are also prohibited, such as treachery or torture of the enemy (the latter being considered as worse than crime), as well as the use of certain weapons causing unnecessary suffering.[133] Enemies who have laid down arms must be spared; those who have fallen in battle must be respected[134], and human remains must be buried.[135] Finally, among the humanitarian terms of Muslim law there is also the fact that armed combat is limited in its duration: an automatic truce interrupts combat for four months of each year.[136] This interruption should enable the warriors to bandage their wounds sustained in combat and to appease the sufferings of the civilian populations.

In their present-day formulation and systematization, the terms of Islamic wartime law are the result of a judicial speculation which was effected two or three centuries after the death of the Prophet. From the beginning of the Arab-Muslim conquest, however, the warriors of Islam adopted a magnificent

---

[128] al-Isra': 33.
[129] ibn-Taimiyyah, *On Public and Private Law*, p. 175.
[130] This is the "call" *da'wah* of Islam.
[131] As a fire or flood which were, at the time of the prophet Muhammad, the means of massive destruction.
[132] Tradition reports that the Prophet raised a prohibition on exporting corn to Makkah.
[133] The Malikiyyah prohibit, for example, poisoned meat. See Khadduri, *War*, p. 103. Also refer to Hamidullah, *Muslim Conduct*, p. 187.
[134] God forbade Muhammad to avenge the memory of his uncle Hamza upon the corpses of the Makkan soldiers.
[135] After the battle of Badr, the Prophet ordered his troops to bury the enemy's dead so that they would not be left as food for lions.
[136] at-Taubah: 36.

46.....................Jihad: A Commitment to Universal Peace

spirit of tolerance toward the nonbelievers and subjugated peoples. At a time when violence knew neither law nor feeling, Abu Bakr, the Prophet's successor, gave his soldiers the following well-known and often-quoted instructions which contain the moral spirit of Islamic law: "Remember that you are always under the gaze of God and at the threshold of your death, and that you will account for your deeds on the Last Day... When you are fighting for the glory of God, acquit yourselves as men, without heaving your backs; but, let not the blood of women, children, or the aged be a blemish on your victory. Do not destroy palm trees, do not burn houses or wheat fields, never cut down fruit trees and do not kill cattle unless you are forced to eat them. When you grant a treaty or a capitulation, take care to fulfill their conditions. As you advance, you will come across religious men who live in monasteries and who serve God in prayer; leave them in peace, do not kill them and do not destroy their monasteries..."[137]

The orders given by Abu Bakr in no way represent pious recommendations. They are strict legal obligations which engage the personal responsibility of the combatant. The soldier of the "holy war" is obliged to present himself "under the gaze of God" sincerely and directly and is subject to the rules of honor and humanity. If strategy – the sign of mastery and intelligence in the art of war[138] – is recommended to him, treachery and trickery are strictly forbidden. The principle of good faith and upright intentions constitutes the moral basis of the Muslim in both combat and all circumstances of his private and public life. Deceit and cheating are condemned as being contrary to the judicial foundations of morality. Certain exceptions are tolerated on the absolute condition that the life of the believer is in extreme danger. However, the limits of moderation always apply. "If you kill, do so in a dignified fashion," said the Prophet. This order is considered by legal doctrine to be the prohibition of treacherous trickery, of torturing the wounded or prisoners, or of killing wounded enemies on the battlefields or leaving them to die by not giving them water or food.

In the same vein of moderation[139] and of respect for man, there is the fact that soldiers of the "holy war" are forbidden to plunder. This prohibition is worth being discussed here, though it could appear secondary in relation to

---

[137]Rabbath, "Pour une théorie," p. 16; and Amir Ali, *Spirit*, pp. 86-87, among others. Abu Zahra cites a tradition attributed to the Prophet: "... Do not kill their old people, the infants or women. Do not be excessive and take care of your spoils; act in the right way and do good ..." (*La conception*, p. 53). See the translation of principal texts reported in Hamidullah, *Muslim Conduct*, pp. 304 f.
[138]Allah Himself is the best in this domain. See al-Anfal: 30.
[139]"He has established the balance. Do not transgress the balance," ar-Rahman: 7-8 (Blachère).

Magnanimity..47

the corpus of Islamic wartime law for it reinforces and illustrates the idea under discussion. The Prophet said: "He who loots or usurps, or who encourages plundering, is not considered as one of us." This prohibition should be placed side by side with the many terms stipulating the rules for sharing booty. It is in this context that the coherence of the revelation and the logic of the prophetic orders become clear. Muhammad actually advised his soldiers who were setting out on a campaign to take care of their booty; according to the Qur'ān, the soldier who is enticed by material gain will not be rewarded: "O you who believe! When you go abroad in the cause of God, investigate carefully, and do not say to anyone who offers you a salutation: 'You are not of the believers,' coveting the perishable goods of this life. With God are profits and spoils abundant."[140] Muslim legalistic literatue, rich in stipulations concerning dividing up booty, imputes numerous declarations to Muhammad in this connection. The great detail with which the doctrine, even from the very outset of Muslim history, treats the distribution of property taken from the enemy constitutes a constraint, a judicial requirement and practice whose strict application, when mutually controlled by all the soldiers, is aimed at preventing the illegal seizing of goods. As such, the innumerable stipulations concerning booty appear to be of secondary importance but represent a practical means of forbidding pillage.

Certain more general terms of Muslim law should be analyzed here. First of all, the enemy must be treated with justice,[141] respect,[142] and compassion.[143] It has been repeated that before battles the Prophet would recite: "O Almighty God. We are your creatures and they are too. Our lives are in Your hands, as are theirs. O God, cause them to be defeated and grant us victory over them." Islamic law which is essentially practical and realistic, does not ask that the combatants "love" their enemy since generosity and charity are impossible without justice. The moderation shown by the Prophet during the conquest of Makkah was not love but magnanimity in his seeking peace and reconciliation. This still does not mean that the enemy is an inferior and damned creature for, like all creatures, he was created by the one God and thus belongs to the brotherhood of men. However, "if humanity unites all men, then truth distinguishes those creatures who submit to obeying God from those who break His laws."[144] Thus, military and wartime commandments

---

[140]an-Nisa': 94 (Masson).
[141]al-Ma'idah: 2.
[142]al-An'am: 109.
[143]al-Baqarah: 195.
[144]Muhammad Z. Khan, "Islam and International Relations," *The Islamic Review* (July 1956):8. After this: Khan, "Islam."

48. .... Jihad: A Commitment to Universal Peace

necessarily imply respect for humanitarian and moral principles. Hostilities are intended to lead to reconciliation; violence has to be checked and limited on personal and geographical levels.

The most obvious originality of the Islamic teaching in the domain of war, is the guarantee offered to noncombatants. This limitation fully corresponds to the spirit of the Qur'ānic revelation which holds man individually responsible; so, the limitation rejoins the concept of "holy war" in Islam, answering those who have taken the initiative of engaging combat. The verse authorizing war is understood and interpreted in these two possible ways. "Fight in the cause of God those who fight you, but do not transgress limits for God does not love transgressors,"[145] means both that war is permitted only to drive back an attack and that Muslim arms must be used only against those who participate in active hostilities. War does not oppose peoples but defenders of faith and those who have attacked them. Therefore, hostilities are limited in their objectives (combatants) and space (the battlefield). Thus, the period of war is reduced.

The Qur'ān not only demands that enemies who do not take part in the combats be shown respect, but that they be shown kindness as well. Women, children, the elderly, religious men, the old and infirm, slaves and servants are protected from any direct attack. The greater part of the legal doctrine seems to extend this protection to adult males who have not had any active part in the hostilities: peasants, workers, merchants, to whose ranks may be added the members of medical and paramedical personnel.[146] In fact, the recognized interpreters of the Qur'ān view the injunction to "help one another with God-fearing kindness"[147] as the duty to cooperate with civilian enemies in humanitarian matters.[148] This is not at all a "modernized" deduction since classical Muslim legal doctrine in effect provided for the permanent neutralization of a health service – women or doctors who were following the wounded[149] of *both* sides.

The prohibition against harming noncombatant civilians implies the ban on certain arms of indiscriminate nature as well as the extent to which the enemy can be harmed. Legal doctrine did not limit itself to expressing a pious oath in this realm but developed precise laws based on plausible examples. By way of illustration, the translation of a legal text relating to Islamic wartime law

---

[145] al-Baqarah: 190 (Blachère). It is convenient to also note that "transgressors" is understood, at the same time, as a prohibition of aggression and a putting on guard against excess.
[146] Muhammad Hamidullah, "The International Law in Islam," *The Islamic Review* (May 1951).
[147] al-Ma'idah: 2.
[148] Hamidullah, *Muslim Conduct*, p. 279.
[149] Khadduri, *The Islamic Law*.

Magnanimity...49

is of significance.[150] The author[151] very explicitly indicates that, for instance, when besieging a fortress in which there are women or children, the Muslims are not allowed to set fire to nor flood the area. "If the enemy surrounds himself with a rampart of children, he must be left alone, unless he proves to be too formidable an enemy." Is this not precisely the practical expression of the necessary compromise between military needs and humanitarian requirements, the basis of modern law applicable in the case of armed conflict?

The distinction between combatants and noncombatants was applied to Muslims themselves, each category having its own obligations. The first category – the soldiers – is "constantly reminded of the religious nature of their mission, that of being a warrior...in [the holy war], for the victory of Allah; from the latter, apart from submission to the authority of Islam, nothing more is required than the strictest neutrality."[152] The concern for separating combatants from noncombatants is moreover witnessed by the soldiers of the first battles of the Prophet who declared: "The factor which distinguishes us from the nonbelievers is the green turban forming part of our headgear."[153]

Civilian citizens of conquered territories fell under the "protection" of Islam. They could continue to live there freely, subject to their own legislation. They ceased to be directly involved with the development of military operations. Rare are the historical examples showing that Jews or Christians had to endure persecution in the form of retaliation, when the tides of fortune would temporarily turn against Muslim powers. Even at the height of the crusades, resident Christians were generally not molested. The few known exceptions were always the deeds of ignorant people. As for nationals of belligerent enemy states who happened to be in Muslim territory during a war, they were permitted to reside there normally until their permit expired. They were to be neither molested, nor threatened in their person or property, nor were they to be expelled or imprisoned, on the condition that they committed no hostile act against Islam.

In the context of the limitation of hostilities, the institution of the safeguard accorded to foreigners, an integral part of the "holy war," should be mentioned again briefly since it offers the possibility of placing limits on the battlefield. This was achieved in two ways. First, thanks to the respect it en-

---

[150]Baron Carra de Vaux, *Les penseurs de l'Islam*, vol. 3: *L'exégèse, la tradition, et la jurisprudence* (Paris: Guenther, 1923), p. 365.
[151]Sidi Khalil of the Malikiyyah.
[152]Rabbath, "Pour une théorie," p. 17.
[153]Hamidullah, *Muslim Conduct*, p. 236. This distinction of the military nature was eventually misinterpreted in order to humiliate those who had surrendered. See below, chapter 5.

50 .... Jihad: A Commitment to Universal Peace

joyed, it must have permitted the establishment of diplomatic channels in order to transmit ultimatums and open negotiations for peace,[154] to communicate the agreement of truces or cease-fires; it also permitted very precise stipulations regulating the conclusion or breaking of treaties. These theoretical hypotheses have very often been put into effect in historical practice and in fact correspond to the modern Islamic spirit and doctrine pertaining to war.[155] Second, during hostilities on the battlefield, there is yet another factor which serves as an obvious limitation on the scope of the conflict: the fact that in the name and upon the responsibility of the entire community, every believer is guaranteed the possibility of granting safeguard to one or several enemies, even if they are situated in fortified positions. This is not a surrender nor even a truce demanded of the enemy. The beneficiaries enjoy this privilege for as long as they abstain from resuming combat. The hostile combatants to whom such a safeguard has been granted do not thereby become prisoners but are permitted to live freely among the Muslims.

Concerning prisoners, the prophetic traditions report the following injunction of Muhammad: "The captives are your brothers and collaborators. It is by God's grace that they are in your hands. Since they are at your mercy, treat them as you treat yourselves with regard to food, clothing, and habitation. Do not demand any work of them which is beyond their capacities, rather, help them to accomplish their tasks." Over and over the Qur'ān mentions that among the actions of great moral value which form an integral part of piety is the kindness which the believer should show toward his captive: "And they feed, for the love of God, the indigent, the orphan, and the captive."[156]

The terms inaugurated by Qur'ānic legislation constitute one of the most lasting and glorious contributions made by Islam to the development of wartime law. Examples of generosity and humanity abound in Muslim history, from Muhammad[157] to Saladin [Salah ud-din] the Great who, according to Arab chroniclers, liberated a great number of crusader prisoners when he realized that he did not have enough food to feed them all.[158] A great deal

---

[154]"If they incline to peace, incline toward them," al-Anfal: 61 (Blachère).
[155]See Abu Zahra, *La conception*; Bêchebichy, *Les relations*; Chalaby, *L'Islam*; and Draz, *Initiation*.
[156]al-Insān: 8 (Blachère).
[157]Tradition reports that the Makkan enemies defeated at the battle of Badr were well treated. At Medinah where they were enemies in captivity, they declared: "Blessed be the people of Medinah. They have given us their horses while they themselves walk. They have given us bread to eat when, haveing little, they content themselves with dates." See Ameer Ali, *The Spirit*, p. 63; Tugay, *Mahomet*, p. 130; and Galwash, *The Religion*, p. 65.
[158]On this very land of Palestine seven centuries later, Napoléon in front of Saint-Jean-d'Acre

Magnanimity..**51**

of original sources mention this fact.

In order to fully comprehend the original and revolutionary aspect of Muhammad's instructions, one has to bear in mind how far back in time they appeared as well as the evolution of morality: this took place in the seventh century at a period when the tradition in Arabia was to ransom one's captives and massacre those who did not have the means to buy their freedom. At the same time, in the West, the "kind" king Dagobert, planting his sword in the ground after battle, had all of the conquered population who were taller than his sword killed."[159]

The Qur'ān,[160] jurisprudence, and historical tradition provide instructions pertaining to the status of prisoners. It should be noted that the doctrine is not always unanimous and does not always seem to conform to Qur'ānic stipulations,[161] nor to the generally followed practices, if we are to believe historians. According to judicial science, it would be up to the leader of the community to decide upon the fate of prisoners. He had four choices: immediate execution, subjection to slavery, ransom and exchange for Muslim prisoners, and finally, unilateral and unconditional liberation. All the Muslim jurists who retain the possibility of immediate execution of a part or all of the prisoners agree in recognizing that this could only be a question of an exceptional measure taken as a military precaution or in the higher interests of society. Nothing in the Qur'ān either prescribes or authorizes the killing of prisoners. The revelation provides for and authorizes only ransom or liberation. The main early legal authority seems to share this opinion.[162] Moreover, historical tradition shows that neither the Prophet nor his successors permitted the execution of prisoners. On the contrary, it would appear that Muhammad's companions and their troops had some difficulties in accepting Islam's humanitarian prescriptions. For example, after the battle of Badr, the first decisive victory of the Muslim forces, those who requested merciful treatment so as to enhance the prestige of Islam and accelerate its propagation[163] were opposed by those who,[164] in the name of simple justice, demanded the execution of the enemies who had apparently shown a particu-

---

massacred all the Syrian prisoners which he detained, by starving them to death. Abu Zahra, *La conception*, p. 63.

[159]Dermenghem, "Témoignage," especially p. 376.

[160][After the capture comes the time for], "... either generosity or ransom until the war lays down its burdens," Muhammad: 4 (Blachère). See also al-Anfal: 70.

[161]Ghoneimi, *The Muslim Conception*, p. 148.

[162]Khadduri, *The Islamic Law*, p. 91, with the simultaneously opposing opinion which is supported, moreover, only by the jurisprudence and that in default with the Qur'ān.

[163]Abu Bakr, who became the first successor.

[164]'Umar, who became the second caliph.

lar violence toward the growing Muslim community. Muhammad decided to free the prisoners for a certain ransom and to keep those who could not pay the price of their liberty. The latter were freed as soon as they had each taught ten children of Medinah to read and write.

Quartering and subjugation of prisoners have, even up to modern times, been a widespread practice. Reducing prisoners to slavery, apart from the fact that it met economic needs, was generally not motivated by humanitarian considerations but rather by the mythical belief that the victors had the right of life and death over them. This custom could have been inherited by Islam from the Persians and Byzantines, with whom the Muslim troops had violent contacts very early on. Tradition reports that Muhammad accepted that the captured enemies be distributed among the believers as slaves, on the strict condition that they be humanely treated, nourished and clothed just like normal citizens, and that they not be subject to excessively difficult tasks.[165] The prophetic traditions also show how the Prophet, without formally forbidding his combatants to subjugate the members of a defeated tribe, encouraged them to free them by marrying one of their women. In this way, they established relationships with the conquered people.[166]

Given the fact that the Qur'ān did not envisage the subjugation of prisoners of war, it seems likely that this measure must have represented only one form of sanction, based on reciprocity. Taking the era into consideration, one could moreover claim that slavery was a lesser evil which allowed for lives to be saved and provided a form of temporary detention. Furthermore, ransom, exchange or liberation were not only possibilities but binding obligations. The precise Qur'ānic commandment – "...until war lays down its burden..." – indicated the time limit of captivity. At the end of the war, all prisoners must necessarily be freed, on the sole condition that the Muslims held captive by the enemy be repatriated at the same time. Maintaining enemy soldiers in captivity nourished the public treasury through ransom and above all offered the possibility of exchanging them for believers as well as non-Muslim subjects who were being held. In the first treaty concluded between Muhammad and the people of Medinah, one clause already stipulates that the allies should not miss any opportunity to recover their imprisoned relatives.[167] The succeeding caliphs insisted that the Muslim administration apply all its efforts in order to recover captured Muslims.

There were also certain legal terms applicable to Muslim soldiers whom the

---

[165]Khan, "Islam," p. 11, who cites al-Bukhari.
[166]This pertains to one of the "political" marriages of the Prophet. See Abu Zahra, *La conception*, p. 73; Hamidullah, *Muslim Conduct*, pp. 216-217; and Tugay, *Mahomet*.
[167]Article 3. See Hamidullah, *The First Written Constitution*, pp. 41-42.

enemy held in captivity. They had to remain faithful to the Islamic faith, and they were formally forbidden to take part in any war against the Muslim community or to provide the enemy with information of a military nature. At the same time, the doctrine considered it the absolute duty of the Muslim leader to obtain their release by means of an exchange of people, properties, or the payment of a ransom. This requirement became a widespread practice.

Islam regulated the conditions and terms of restitution by means of specific treaties called *fida*. The frequency of battles between Islam and the outside world made this an almost routine procedure. This fact had no small influence in saving thousands of lives and in ensuring the safeguard of those enemy soldiers which warfare had put out of combat.[168] It moreover enabled medieval Europe to become aware of the state of prisoners in the East, whose retrieval then became possible.

Cases of unconditional liberation are not rare in Muslim history. The best-known examples are, first of all, the Prophet's unconditional liberation of all prisoners captured when Makkah was taken, and Saladin who released the Christians who had no means of buying their freedom when the Muslim armies retook Jerusalem.

Taking into account the absolute word of the Qur'ān and the spirit of the Islamic revelation, contemporary Muslim jurists consider that the only possible alternative for the Muslim leader is either to unilaterally liberate the prisoners whom he holds captive, or to exchange them for Muslim prisoners who are in the hands of the enemy or against a certain ransom. This is the interpretation which seems to be the most appropriate in terms of the causes, limitations, and aims of the "holy war" in Islam.

Eternal Principles

Asserting the oneness of God, truth, and the human race, Islam immediately appeared as an ecumenical religion and a political system of universal aims. Since it simultaneously recognized the authenticity of the preceding divine revelations, it conceived of the universe as a single entity having a pluralistic formation. It then came to the point of defining itself in relation to the outside world, thereby giving rise to a bipolar conception of the universe. This division is not based upon geographical or juridical criteria but represents a state to be described rather than a situation which could be subjectively judged, since it emanates from the divine will.

---

[168] Khadduri, *War*, p. 217, notes that these treaties of exchange were numerous mainly during the Abbassid period. Twelve treaties of ransom or of exchange are known in only the first years of the reign of Harun ar-Rashid.

54. .... Jihad: A Commitment to Universal Peace

The Muslim world, ruled by Qur'ānic legislation, concretely represents the domain of justice and peace, the *world of Islam*; whereas the exterior countries, if certain conditions are not fulfilled, remain the sphere of oppression and error, the *world of war*. This (latter) world is hostile toward Islam insofar as the believers residing there have neither freedom of conscience nor security of their persons or belongings. Thus, injustice and violence are apprehended from within. The two systems are irrevocably separated by this inherent clash which makes them mutually exclusive. However, the objective division of the world exists in order to encourage men to cooperate and to avoid the exclusive domination of one political entity over the others since God desires harmony and fraternity among peoples.

Peace in justice is the deepest essence of the Islamic revelation. The prophetic tradition reports in this connection that once, in answer to a question, the Prophet defined the "best Islam" as that which "consisted of feeding those who are hungry and of spreading peace among the known and the unknown" [i.e., between believers and nonbelievers] of the whole world.[169] By force of circumstances, and particularly because of its geographical location, the Muslim community was soon compelled to define and maintain neighborly relations based on peaceful coexistence. Rules appeared to determine the terms of these relations. International relations were supposed to remain peaceful as long as the outside world had an agreeable and tolerant attitude.[170] If the universe necessarily had to be divided into two "domains" eternally hostile toward each other because of belief, neutrality would have been inconceivable. However, there is nothing which opposes the idea of a third party remaining uninvolved in hostilities. Accordingly, the Qur'ān forbids Muslims to attack a nation which has not shown any hostility toward them, providing all the guarantees of security.[171]

Islam of course turned out to be proselytic. The nature of its external relations was largely determined by the objective reality of various eras, political ambitions of certain leaders, and strength of arms. On a strictly religious level, these relations should have been characterized by moderation and patience. As the "midway nation," the Muslim community had to accept and acknowledge the existence of other peoples ruled by different laws. Since law is "personalized," the foreigner was able to reside in Islamic territory, permanently or temporarily, adhering to his own laws. Reciprocally, the Muslim

---

[169]Goldziher, *Le dogme*, p. 18.
[170]Hassan al-Ma'amoun, "Quelques principes de l'Islam," *Revue internationale de la Croix-Rouge*, November 1958, p. 598.
[171]an-Nisa': 90.

Eternal Principles...55

who entered the "world of war" was obliged to respect the public order of that place. On the level of interstate relations, right from its inception, the Muslim state maintained diplomatic relations with the outside world. However, the profound sense of justice as well as the dynamic and collective apprehension of the concept of compassion encourage the Muslim to reduce the "world of disorder and oppression" to nonexistence. The instrument of this procedure is the *jihad*.

The "holy war" is an effort. First, it is an effort made to curb the passions of the self; an effort which is also communal so as to enforce good and forbid evil; it is finally an armed effort imposed upon the believer individually or upon the community as a whole, as circumstances may require. Its aim is not to impose Islam but to maintain the society's security and to ensure its expansion by making sure that anybody outside of the world of Islam is free to embrace the faith. Nonbelief is punishment in itself. The nonbeliever who does not prevent Muslims from practicing their faith is in need of no other punishment.[172] The "holy war" could not assume a military character other than within the confines determined by Qur'ānic law. It then becomes armed aggression, holy and pious, just in its motivation, waging, and end. Since the traditional doctrine considers aggression a natural trait of man, it describes as iniquitous those conflicts whose motivation lies in the desire for revenge, in rivalry of personal interests and jealousy, as well as in the "tendency for violence or vandalism."[173] The only just wars are those authorized by the revelation and fought "in the path of Allah." Any other form of violence is condemned. In the final analysis, force should theoretically lead back to the existential unity desired by God; to order and harmony, to "soundness," to justice in its broadest meaning. In this nonmilitary context, the "holy war" is a permanent state since man is created in such a way that he must constantly be harsh with himself and others in order to fight his natural tendencies toward selfishness, injustice, and desire for power.

Islam's military history is woven of superior military deeds, of examples of tolerance and magnanimity, as well as of massacres. It is a history of men. The Muslims of today are not wrong in proudly looking back on their past. The Prophet and his successors – in particular the caliph Umar, the great empire builder – succeeded in using Islam to inculcate respect for man and recognition of human values in their combatants, the enthusiastic zealots of a

---

[172]"Be that as it may, the unbeliever who does not forbid to the Muslims to establish the religion of Allah has himself already suffered the disadvantages of his unbelief." ibn-Taimiyyah, *On Public Law*, p. 141.
[173]The raids of razzia. See ibn-Khaldoun, *Mouqaddima*, pp. 56 f.

56. . . . . Jihad: A Commitment to Universal Peace

new religion.[174] The extraordinary examples of humanity shown by – among others – Muhammad at the time of the conquest of Makkah, 'Umar when he rode into Jerusalem, and Saladin in various circumstances during his struggle with the crusaders, incessantly return under the pen of Muslim authors, historians, jurists, or moralists. With the internal dissensions and wars which soon arose, followed in Spain and the Levant by the brutal contact with a Europe which was beginning to stir, the necessities of the moment led to excesses. The invasion of Turkish tribes from the West and then the terrifying waves of Mongols nevertheless did not bring much damage to the Islamic concept of war on the level of doctrine.[175] To claim that all Muslim leaders followed the legal terms governing international relations – both during times of peace and war – would be to display an ignorance of the history of human nature. These violations all the same do not diminish the value of the religious laws which remain immutable. A contravention of the law takes nothing away from its obligating and coercive nature.

Simultaneously based on the concepts of force and compassion, the fundamental principles of the Islamic legal system pertaining to both interstate and internal conflicts may be summed up as follows:[176]

– Prohibition of excess, treachery, and injustice in all areas.
– Prohibition of inflicting unnecessary suffering upon the enemy: no massacres, cruelty, or vindictive punishment.
– Prohibition of uncalled-for destruction, in particular the devastation of civilizations.
– Condemnation of poisoned weapons or of mass and indiscriminate destruction.
– Clear distinctions between the combatants, who in Muslim armies wore a distinctive insignia, and civilians not directly participating in combat.

---

[174]We emphasize, at this stage, that the rules of the law of war do not represent a myth "modernized" by the contemporary Muslim authors who try to prove the concordance of the religion with the present juridical principles. The apostolic tradition is rich in examples. In the fourteenth century, a chronicler compiling the reported anecdotes mentions the recommendations of Muhammad as regards the treatment of prisoners and lets his readers perceive the indignation of the Muslims when coming across their Arab enemies finishing off the wounded on the battlefield. See ibn-Sayed al-Nass, "Des anciennes sources de combat, du comportement des guerriers, et de leur bibliographie" [On the Ancient Sources Concerning Combat, the Behavior of Warriors, and on their Bibliography] in Farag al-Sayed, *Message au soldat arabe* [Message to the Arab Soldier], translated by Mohamed Nasr al-Dine (Cairo: Supreme Council of Islamic Affairs, n.d.), pp. 43, 63. After this: al-Sayed, *Message.*

[175]See the analysis for another period by Sivan Emmanuel, *L'Islam et la Croisace: Idéologie et propagande dans les réactions musulmanes aux Croisades* (Paris: Maisonneuve, 1968), 222 pages. After this: Sivan, *Idéologie et propagande.*

Eternal Principles. **57**

- Respect for those who have withdrawn from battle: the wounded, soldiers granted free passage – safeguard – and prisoners of war.
- Humane treatment of captives who must be exchanged or unilaterally freed when the war comes to an end, on the condition that there remain no Muslim prisoners in the hands of the enemy.
- Protection of civilian populations: respect for their religions – and hence their cultures – and the ministers of the latter; prohibition of murder of hostages or rape of women.
- Affirmation of individual responsibility: abolition of any punishment of persons for a crime which they have not committed themselves.
- Prohibition of reciprocity in inflicting suffering and retaliation which could constitute a contravention of essential human rights.
- Collaboration with the enemy in humanitarian tasks.
- Formal prevention of any act contrary to the stipulations of treaties concluded by the Muslims.

Because they consider the law to be of divine essence, Muslim jurists go by a certain number of idealized norms, refusing to codify practices which could be legal tender. With regard to armed combat, Islam – which may claim the honor of never having known systematic genocide nor concentration camps – proclaims universal rules. It is thus endowed with moderation and wisdom such as could benefit mankind at the present time. All excesses are banned in the name of justice and reason. War is not an act of revenge, but an effort to drive out iniquity and oppression. This is a concept which poses very precise restrictions as to the manner of carrying out military operations, a notion which proceeds from a higher conception of man as such and from the respect due to him as a creature of God. Islamic international law reposes upon solid moral principles which aim to transcend the everyday human reality. The Prophet Muhammad declared this most explicitly: "God Almighty sent me to perfect your character and to make it more dignified."

---

[176] We again take up here the ideas already developed in our short article: "De certaines règles islamiques concernant la conduite des hostilités et la protection des victimes de conflits armés," Annales d'études internationales, 1977), pp. 145-158.